Resurrecting the Republic

by

Charles L. Perry

Introduction

This book is written from necessity. With my being just an average citizen of this country makes me aware of what is going on inside our government. All the people I socialize with seem to agree that there is something drastically wrong with the way our country is being managed. Using my powers of observation brings me to the realization that there are more people out there who feel the same way that my circle of friends do. Hence the demand for a solution to this dilemma, what can we do to remedy this conundrum?

Be sure of one thing, I love this country. I love it so much that I put my life on the line to protect it. I did the job for 22 years and loved it.

As I said, I am just a concerned citizen, however, through observation and training I have developed a solution for repairing this horrendous situation. Is what I'm suggesting the only answer? No.

I'm sure there are many other ideas that may or may not work satisfactorily. Even if there are other ways, that is not to say that my way shouldn't be considered. So I have written this book to that response.

As to my background, I am a retired military type. Spent 22 years in the Marine Corps and Navy and thoroughly enjoyed most of my career. While in the Military I availed myself of the educational system and acquired 2 degrees, one in Business Management, the other a Master's Degree in Human Resources Management. After getting out of the Military I spent a portion of my useful life teaching College students. Trying to pass on what I had learned from my life. As I said, I'm just an ordinary guy doing ordinary things.

It almost seems to me that when I decided to retire that my retirement caused the collapse of the United States economy. I know it didn't, but it sure seemed like that to me. Anyway, because I'm retired I now have time to look at what is happening with our system of governance and our economic system. They are both in total disarray. And I know why!

What became apparent to me was that Government is nothing more than a Business, and if we want to make government function for our good (as mentioned by Aristotle) then we should manage it the same way we would if it was a profitable business. By doing so we could make government operate for our benefit. So that is what this offering is, a way to restructure our Governmental System into a system that if it were a business would be run efficiently and profitably. At the very least we can reorganize the system to work efficiently and get things done in a sensible way. As it stands now it's being run through greed and deceit. We all know what goes on up there in Congress today. Did you know during WWII the government hired the Mafia to help win the war. What kind of integrity is that?

One of the main problems with the machinations of the government now is that it is too old. (It's known that most governmental systems only last about 200 years.) When we look at a business, we see that every so often a critical look must be taken about where the business is and if it needs to be changed. These changes can happen due to competition, a change in Management or a shift in technology. Unfortunately our government has no competition; therefore there is no one to give us a standard by which to judge ourselves to keep it running as it should. Our government is way past the time when it should be looking at its system operation and trying to see if there should be some changes.

In this book I will delineate the steps required to get the government back on track, the way our forefathers had intended it to be.

Foreword

Just take a look at what's happening today.

There are businesses failing in record numbers. There are less and less job opportunities, with more and more social unrest. What do we have at our disposal to deal during these disastrous times?   Gas…$3.59 per gallon or more depending on what time of the year it is, and where in the US you are. Green Peppers $1.00 each, more homes in foreclosure than at any time in our history, and taxes going through the roof. No one I have talked to is willing to say that it's going to get better any time soon.

We have only to look at our own history to see the answer. These are the same grievances that our Forefathers experienced when they chose to gather together and form a Republic.

We are much more fortunate than they were…we have some good documentation on how it should be done. Our Forefathers not only gave us their historical data, but they also left behind a set of rules with which to resurrect our lost Republic.

That's right we have the tools within the Constitution to get it done. All we need to do is handle it wisely and we can get ourselves back on track as the most successful government on earth. Now's the time for us to seriously get started on this process. We need to bring about this rebirth now, before our country sinks beneath the waves like the European continent has done. With my plan we can be the forerunner of the ultimate fix for the politics and economy not only for our country but for the world. I mean, really don't we want to be the leaders rather than the followers in this world reformation.

This book provides the answer for that to happen. It won't be easy, nor will it happen overnight, but if we want it to get done we <u>must get started!</u>

Table of Contents

List of References for Research

Chapter 1 – History of the Republic

www.wikipedia.org -
http://creativecommons.org/licenses/by-sa/3.0/
Declaration of Independence
Preamble to the Constitution of the United
States
Standard Encyclopedia of Philosophy
Aristotle
Cicero

Chapter 2 – Why a Republic

www.wikipedia.org -
http://creativecommons.org/licenses/by-
sa/3.0/
First Constitution – Articles of
Confederation and Perpetual Union
First Declaration of Independence
Constitutional Convention
The Constitution of the United States of
America
Article 10

Charter 3 – The Inevitable Death of the Federal Government

www.wikipedia.org - http://creativecommons.org/licenses/by-sa/3.0/
Prohibition in the United States

Chapter 4 – How do we start

www.ed.gov
Article written by Christine Lagorio released by the AP September 13th 2005

Chapter 5 – All Business has a useful life
www.wikipedia.org - http://creativecommons.org/licenses/by-sa/3.0/
IBM historical archives

Chapter 6 – Machinations of the Resurrection - none

Chapter 7 – What's the Fix

www.gpo.gov
Federal Budget

www.wikipedia.org - http://creativecommons.org/licenses/by-sa/3.0/
Taxes

Chapter 1 - History of the Republic

When the United States was born, we were organized by our founding fathers using the governmental theory based on a Republic. The definition of a republic is a form of government in which the people or some portion thereof have supreme control over the government, and in which the head of government is not a king or monarch. That is the premise we will examine in this book. Assuming the majority of the people in the US still believe in the idea of people controlling the government, we will examine if, in fact, we are still operating under the ideals of a republic and if not, can we recover that ideal and if we can…how.

The word "republic" is derived from the Latin phrase *res publica*, which can be translated as "a public affair". This Republican method of choice was predictable, as the United States was attempting to divest itself from the dictatorial rule of a monarchy and with the misuse they had suffered under this form of oppressive control still resounding in their heads, an alternative form would necessarily be preferable. The Colonists were adamant about entering into a "self-rule" method whereby the common populace had a major say on the determinants of government. By selecting the Republican form, the people of the US were trying to avoid the oppression of the past, by putting their governance unto themselves. They did however adopt a style similar to Great Britain that being a Parliamentary form of Government. The basic make-up being that of an executive branch, a judicial branch and a legislative or congressional branch. The major difference was the executive branch which would not be controlled by a monarch, rather by an elected president.

These similarities in form are again the most obvious for the colonists to choose because this is the form in which they were raised and with which they had become most comfortable. Through critical thinking they chose what they determined to be the most efficient system for their needs. Their decisions were made to comply with the theories of Aristotle and Cicero while keeping the structure of their system up to date for the time.

What transpired was an august governmental system that was fraught with wisdom and flexibility. The challenge we have today is generally not with what our forefathers organized for us, but with what the greedy "professional" politicians have since concocted for their own devices and for their ill-gotten gains which have become a major detriment to our governmental system. The main problem we have now is undoing the wrongs these "professional" ogres have perpetrated upon us.

The concept of the "republic" first began in prehistoric times. The concept began simply as a protection methodology for a group of people endeavoring to survive in a violent world. Being one of the weakest beings on the planet it was soon known that for us to survive, humans needed some help. So, we learned that help could be garnered through grouping together. Through trial and error it was discovered there was safety in numbers. This grouping together in loosely bound social associations afforded individuals more security and a more prosperous life. From this idea of prosperity through social organization came the two basic forms of governance, the monarchy and the republic. There are two states of the classical era that are today by convention called republics. These include the city states of ancient Greece such as Athens and Sparta and the Roman Republic. There are other examples but for our purpose these two will be the standard by which we measure the US republic. Although the structure and governance of these states was very different from that of any modern republic, we will look at both the similarities and the differences.

The political philosophy of the classical republics has had a central influence on republican thought throughout the subsequent centuries. A number of classical writers discussed forms of government that were alternatives to monarchies and later writers have treated these as foundational works on the nature of republics. Aristotle's *Politics* discusses various forms of government. One form Aristotle named *politeia* consisted of a mixture of the other forms. He argued this was one of the ideal forms of government. Polybius expanded on many of these ideas, again focusing on the idea of **diverse government**. The most important Roman work in this tradition is Cicero's *De Re Publica*.

Although experts say the ideas and theories of the ancients are not of use in our concepts of modern republics it may be useful to again look at the cradle of our political thought; where it started and their basic use to formulate these ideas.

Aristotle's Political Theory

(from Wikipedia - the "Stanford Encyclopedia of Philosophy

First published Wed Jul 1, 1998; substantive revision Fri Jul 19, 2002

Aristotle (b. 384 - d. 322 BC), was a Greek philosopher, logician, and scientist. Along with his teacher Plato, Aristotle is generally regarded as one of the most influential ancient thinkers in a number of philosophical fields, including political theory. Aristotle was born in Stagira in northern Greece, and his father was a court physician to the king of Macedon. As a young man he studied in Plato's Academy in Athens. After Plato's death he left Athens to conduct philosophical and biological research in Asia Minor and Lesbos, and he was then invited by King Philip II of Macedon to tutor his young son, Alexander the Great. Soon after Alexander succeeded his father, consolidated the conquest of the Greek city-states, and launched the invasion of the Persian Empire. Aristotle returned as a resident alien to Athens, and was a close friend of Antipater the Macedonian viceroy. At this time (335-323 BC) he wrote or at least completed some of his major treatises, including the *Politics*. When Alexander died suddenly, Aristotle had to flee from Athens because of his Macedonian connections, and he died soon after. Aristotle's life seems to have influenced his political thought in various ways: his interest in biology seems to be expressed in the naturalism of his politics; his interest in comparative politics and his sympathies for democracy as well as monarchy may have been encouraged by his travels and experience of diverse political systems; he criticizes harshly, while borrowing extensively, from Plato's *Republic*, *Statesman*, and *Laws*; and his own *Politics* is intended to guide rulers and statesmen, reflecting the high political circles in which he moved.

"Politics is a practical science, since it is concerned with the noble action or happiness of the citizens (although it resembles a <u>productive science</u> in that it seeks to create, preserve, and reform political systems." Aristotle thus understands politics as a normative or prescriptive discipline rather than as a purely empirical or descriptive inquiry.

In *Nicomachean Ethics*, Aristotle characterizes politics as the most authoritative science. It prescribes which sciences are to be studied in the city-state, and the other capacities -- such as military science, household management, and rhetoric (speaking or writing persuasively) -- fall under its authority. Since it governs the other practical sciences, their ends serve as means to its end, which is nothing less than the human good. "Even if the end is the same for an individual and for a city-state, that of the city-state seems at any rate greater and more complete to attain and preserve. For although it is worthy to attain it for only an individual, it is nobler and more divine to do so for a nation or city-state." Aristotle's political science encompasses the two fields which modern philosophers distinguish as ethics and political philosophy. Political philosophy in the narrow

sense is roughly speaking the subject of his treatise called the *Politics*.
(Excerpt from a dissertation on Aristotle's *Politics)*

One can also explain the existence of the city-state in terms of the four causes. It is a kind of community, that is, a collection of parts having some functions and interests in common. Hence, it is made up of parts, which Aristotle describes in various ways in different contexts: as households, or economic classes (e.g., the rich and the poor), or demes (i.e., local political units). But, ultimately, the city-state is composed of individual citizens, who, along with natural resources, are the "material" or "equipment" out of which the city-state is fashioned.

The formal cause of the city-state is its constitution (*politeia*). Aristotle defines the constitution as "a certain ordering of the inhabitants of the city-state". He also speaks of the constitution of a community as "the form of the compound" and argues that whether the community is the same over time depends on whether it has the same constitution. The constitution is not a written document, but an immanent organizing principle, ***analogous to the soul of an organism***. Hence, the **constitution is also "the way of life" of the citizens**. Here the citizens are that minority of the resident population who are adults with full political rights (e.g. authorized voters).

The existence of the city-state also requires an efficient cause, namely, its ruler. In Aristotle's view, a community of any sort can possess order only if it has a ruling element or authority. This ruling principle is defined by the constitution, which sets criteria for political offices, particularly the sovereign office. However, on a deeper level, there must be an efficient cause to explain why a city-state acquires its constitution in the first place.

Aristotle states that "the person who first established (the city-state) is the cause of very great benefits". This person was evidently the lawgiver, someone like Solon of Athens or Lycurgus of Sparta, who founded the constitution. Aristotle compares the lawgiver, or the politician more generally, to a craftsman like a weaver or shipbuilder, who fashions material into a finished product.

The notion of final cause dominates Aristotle's *Politics* from the opening lines:

"Since we see that every city-state is a sort of community and that every community is established for the sake of some good (for everyone does everything for the sake of what they believe to be good), it is clear that every community aims at some good, and the community which has the most authority of all and includes all the others aims highest, that is, at the good with the most authority. This is what is called the city-state or political community."

Soon after, he states that the city-state comes into being for the sake of life but exists for the sake of the good life. The theme that the good life or happiness is the proper end of the city-state recurs throughout the *Politics*. Another point to pay attention to is, **"For although it is worthy to attain it for only an individual, it is nobler and more divine to do so for a nation or city-state."** So what he alludes to here is that the larger government, even though it is attentive to the individual it is not fashioned towards the individual it is organized for the common good, or to put it another way, for the majority. (This is of particular importance today, because we seem to have strayed away from this premise that we should govern for the majority and have drifted to governing instead for the minority).

To sum up, the city-state is a hylomorphic (i.e., matter-form) compound of a particular population (i.e., citizen-body) in a given territory (material cause) and a constitution (formal cause). The constitution itself is fashioned by the lawgiver and is governed by politicians, who are like craftsmen (efficient cause), and the constitution defines the aim of the city-state (final cause.)

It is in these terms that Aristotle understands the fundamental normative problem of politics: What constitutional form should the lawgiver and politician establish and preserve in what material for the sake of what end?

So here we see the initial philosophy of the republic. A "City-State"(I.E. Our Federal government) the form, for a particular population (the citizens of the United States) using a constitution that is fashioned by lawgivers and governed by politicians for the benefit (good) of the citizens (final cause). That sounds like a good basic premise for the foundation of a government. Let's look at this as a place to start looking at the change needed for the "benefit of the populace (e.g. the voting majority).

Cicero's De Re Publica

The second ancient republic worth examining is the republic of Rome. Most scholars agree to be the most learned treatise on the Romans republican ideas is Cicero's De Re Publica.

Marcus Tullius Cicero (106–43 BCE) was the most famous "new man" of Roman politics, hailing from a minor provincial landowning family rather than the great clans of hereditary nobility. He rose to the office of consul and the Senatorial membership it conferred by his wits and audacity as a lawyer and orator in public prosecutions. His greatest moment as consul in 63 BC came in exposing a conspiracy by Catiline; his brutal suppression of the conspiracy, executing Roman citizens without trial, although a great achievement it would however mar his political legacy. He became an enemy of Julius Caesar (though accepting a pardon from him at the end of a stretch of civil wars in 47 BC), seeing the assertion of rule by first Caesar and then Marc Antony as fatal to the republic. Having defended in his *De officiis* the murder of Caesar in 44 BC, Cicero was himself murdered a year later by partisans of the then-ruling Triumvirate in which Antony figured.

De Re Publica was composed by Cicero between 54 and 51 BC, a turbulent period of strife in Roman politics. Its dramatic setting is in 129 BC at time of the crisis caused by Tiberius Gracchus, a consul who had championed a property redistribution law for the people and whom the Senate had suppressed as a threat to Roman civil order. All of it except the "Dream of Scipio" (Book VI) was lost from the Middle Ages onward; it has been reconstructed from references and excerpts in later authors, supplemented by a palimpsest of much of Books I-III discovered in 1819. Framed as a dialogue between Scipio Aemilianus, a hero of the anti-Gracchi resistance, and several others of his actual contemporaries, the dialogue has a discernible structure as identified by E.M. Atkins (2000: 490): Books I-II treat "the best condition of the *res publica*"; Books III-IV treat "justice and human nature", topics common to the best city and the best citizen; and Books V-VI treat the "best citizen' in the discussion of the statesman and in the Dream of Scipio.

While justice was for Cicero, as for the Greeks, the fundamental bond of the commonwealth, he offered distinctive and influential linked definitions of the *res publica* ("commonwealth", but literally the "public thing") as the *res populi*, the "property/thing of the people", and of a *populus* or "people" in turn as "an assemblage associated with one another by agreement on law [*iuris consensu*] and community of interest [*utilitatis communione*]" (both, I.39). This could be interpreted either as a strong normative claim –*the people agree on law*, also translatable as right or justice, and share a common interest – or in a weaker deflationary manner, in which the people nominally accept a common law and share a common conception of their self-interest which may or may not be in accord with justice. Such ambiguity would be famously exploited by Augustine, who used Cicero's definition to argue that lacking justice, conflicted and divided republican Rome had been no commonwealth, before offering his own even weaker definition of a "people" as those united in (any) common love. In Cicero's own hands, the definitions were used to stress that **the commonwealth was the property of the people, who entrusted it to the magistrates to be used for the common good, and that the "welfare of the people is the supreme law"** ("salus populi suprema lex", this was a reference to a maxim in the ancient "Twelve Tables" compendium of Roman law). It followed too that just as Plato denied the title of a (single unified) regime to the imperfect regimes torn by civil discord, so Cicero inferred that corrupt regimes were not strictly speaking *res publicae* at all. **The role of the statesman (*rector rei publicae*) is to aim at the happiness of the citizens, defined in a laxer way than most Greek philosophers would allow, as wealth, glory, and virtue all combined.**

Cicero's spokesman Scipio adheres to Greek philosophical principles in declaring that **"the commonwealth cannot possibly function without justice"**, adhering to the standard abstract definition in an Aristotelian vein of justice as "giving each their due" (*ius suum cuique tribuere*). In Book III, two other dialogue participants present respectively the famous arguments given on one day for justice, and on the next day against justice, by the skeptical Greek philosopher and ambassador to Rome Carneades. Cicero's presentation reverses the order, no doubt to give justice the last word.

In Cicero's hands, Carneades' case against justice avails itself of the *nomos/phusis* contrast and of the kind of ambition for power expressed by Plato's character Callicles in the *Gorgias*. Justice is not natural, as it differs radically among different peoples; it conflicts with wisdom, which tells us "to rule over as many people as possible, to enjoy pleasures, to be powerful, to rule, to be a lord", and it is fatal for states and empires, which can't survive without injustice. The speech for justice avails itself in contrast of Stoic themes: "true law is right reason, consonant with nature"; there is "one eternal and unchangeable law" [i.e. what has come to be known as "natural law"]. This includes rule of the best over the weakest for the benefit of the latter: as in Plato's *Republic*, the justice of rulership is not exploitation but paternalistic benefit. And as in Plato's Book X, where the myth of Er supplies a revisionary religious justification for justice (it will help you to choose your next reincarnation well), so Cicero's *Republic* concludes with a dream recounted by Scipio Aemilianus about his even more eminent Roman ancestor, Scipio Africanus. The dream describes the divine order which both rewards humans for just service to their city, and also puts human affairs in a cosmic perspective designed not to humble humans but to embolden them to care more for justice than for petty human advantage: you must always look at these heavenly bodies and scorn what is human. What fame can you achieve in what men say, or what glory can you achieve that is worth seeking?"

In a dramatic rejection even of the traditional Roman motive of honor and glory as a motivation to virtue, the imagined elder statesman asks: "…and even the people who talk about us—how long will they do that?"

Looking at Cicero, his writings and his manipulations of the Roman Republic, what are we able to glean from this historical happenstance? **Cicero observed *"the people agree on law"*, and *"share a common interest"*, these statements seem to say the people (I.E. the majority of the people) need to agree on how they will be governed.** That statement, when looked at within the context of our Constitution, agrees with our country's original intent. Another part of the treatise states, *the commonwealth was the property of the people, who entrusted it to the magistrates to be used for the common good, and that the "welfare of the people is the supreme law"* So according to

22

Cicero, his observation was that the commonwealth (Government) was the property of the people, who, in turn, entrusted (assigned the responsibility of running) to the magistrates (politicians) to be used for the common good (the good of the majority) and that the "welfare of the people is the supreme law"! (again comes up the ideal that this government **MUST** be run for the benefit of the majority of the people.) He further explains more distinctly, "***the justice of rulership is not exploitation but paternalistic benefit.***" This implies the ideal of good parental leadership. Not a leadership who is manipulating their position for personal gain, but instead, using it for the good of the majority of the people.

Over time the classical republics were either conquered by empires or became one, themselves. Most of the Greek republics were absorbed into the Macedonian Empire of Alexander. The Roman Republic expanded by conquering the other states around the Mediterranean. The Roman Republic itself then became the Roman Empire and finally the Holy Roman Empire.

Must we endure the same fate? I propose to you, if we do not change our methodologies and rhetoric, we will, inevitably live out the same historical story.

Modern and ancient republics vary considerably in their ideology and composition. The most common definition of a republic is a state without a monarch. In republics such as the United States and France, the executive is legitimized both by a Constitution and by popular support of the people. In the United States, James Madison defined *republic* in terms of a representative democracy , and this usage is still employed by many viewing themselves as "democrats". Montesquieu (in France) included both democracies, where all the people have a share in rule, and aristocracies or oligarchies, where only some of the people rule, as republican forms of government. In modern political science, republicanism refers to a specific set of tenets that are based on good civic quality and are considered distinct from ideas such as liberalism. But our case remains unsolved. Do we continue on the road to our demise or do we institute some form of change to reinvigorate our system and move on with the gusto we once enjoyed? I will attempt to propose a possible solution to that conundrum in this book.

The actual situation we are experiencing now is precisely the same as what our forefathers experienced under British rule. So, in order to decide what we should do about our current situation we need only go to our original Declaration of Independence.

In the Preamble, which was written by John Adams, begins by saying: Whereas his Britannic Majesty, in conjunction with the lords and commons of Great Britain, has, by a late act of Parliament, excluded the inhabitants of these United Colonies from the protection of his crown; And whereas, no answer, whatever, to the humble petitions of the colonies for redress of grievances and reconciliation with Great Britain, has been or is likely to be given; but, the whole force of that kingdom, aided by foreign mercenaries, is to be exerted for the destruction of the good people of these colonies; And whereas, it appears absolutely irreconcilable to reason and good Conscience, for the people of these colonies now to take the oaths and affirmations necessary for the support of any government under the crown of Great Britain, and it is necessary that the exercise of every kind of authority under the said crown should be totally suppressed, and all the powers of government exerted, under the authority of the people of the colonies, for the preservation of internal peace, virtue, and good order, as well as for the defense of their lives, liberties, and properties, against the hostile invasions and cruel depredations of their enemies; therefore, resolved, &c.

Sounds like a Divorce decree doesn't it? But if we look at this preamble critically we will see that with only a few minor changes, like inserting our own federal government where they put the British crown our forefathers are trying to address the same situations we have with our government today. And it continues…

IN CONGRESS, July 4, 1776.

The unanimous Declaration of the thirteen united States of America,

When in the Course of human events, it becomes necessary for one people to dissolve the political bands which have connected them with another, and to assume among the powers of the earth, the separate and equal station to which the Laws of Nature and of Nature's God entitle them, a decent respect to the opinions of mankind requires that they should declare the causes which impel them to the separation.

We hold these truths to be self-evident, that all men are created equal, that they are endowed by their Creator with certain unalienable Rights, that among these are Life, Liberty and the pursuit of Happiness.--That to secure these rights, Governments are instituted among Men, deriving their just powers from the consent of the governed, --That whenever any Form of Government becomes destructive of these ends, it is the Right of the People to alter or to abolish it, and to institute new Government, laying its foundation on such principles and organizing its powers in such form, as to them shall seem most likely to effect their Safety and Happiness. Prudence, indeed, will dictate that Governments long established should not be changed for light and transient causes; and accordingly all experience hath shewn, that mankind are more disposed to suffer, while evils are sufferable, than to right themselves by abolishing the forms to which they are accustomed. But when a long train of abuses and usurpations, pursuing invariably the same Object evinces a design to reduce them under absolute Despotism, it is their right, it is their duty, to throw off such Government, and to provide new Guards for their future security.--Such has been the patient sufferance of these Colonies; and such is now the necessity which constrains them to alter their former Systems of Government. The history of the present King of Great Britain is a history of repeated injuries and usurpations, all having in direct object the establishment of an absolute Tyranny over these States. To prove this, let Facts be submitted to a candid world.

He has refused his Assent to Laws, the most wholesome and necessary for the public good.
He has forbidden his Governors to pass Laws of immediate and pressing importance, unless suspended in their operation till his Assent should be obtained; and when so suspended, he has utterly neglected to attend to them.
He has refused to pass other Laws for the accommodation of large districts of people, unless those people would relinquish the right of Representation in the Legislature, a right inestimable to them and formidable to tyrants only.

He has called together legislative bodies at places unusual, uncomfortable, and distant from the depository of their public Records, for the sole purpose of fatiguing them into compliance with his measures.

He has dissolved Representative Houses repeatedly, for opposing with manly firmness his invasions on the rights of the people.

He has refused for a long time, after such dissolutions, to cause others to be elected; whereby the Legislative powers, incapable of Annihilation, have returned to the People at large for their exercise; the State remaining in the mean time exposed to all the dangers of invasion from without, and convulsions within.

He has endeavoured to prevent the population of these States; for that purpose obstructing the Laws for Naturalization of Foreigners; refusing to pass others to encourage their migrations hither, and raising the conditions of new Appropriations of Lands.

He has obstructed the Administration of Justice, by refusing his Assent to Laws for establishing Judiciary powers.

He has made Judges dependent on his Will alone, for the tenure of their offices, and the amount and payment of their salaries.

He has erected a multitude of New Offices, and sent hither swarms of Officers to harrass our people, and eat out their substance.

He has kept among us, in times of peace, Standing Armies without the Consent of our legislatures.

He has affected to render the Military independent of and superior to the Civil power.

He has combined with others to subject us to a jurisdiction foreign to our constitution, and unacknowledged by our laws; giving his Assent to their Acts of pretended Legislation:

For Quartering large bodies of armed troops among us:

For protecting them, by a mock Trial, from punishment for any Murders which they should commit on the Inhabitants of these States:

For cutting off our Trade with all parts of the world:

For imposing Taxes on us without our Consent:

For depriving us in many cases, of the benefits of Trial by Jury:

For transporting us beyond Seas to be tried for pretended offences

For abolishing the free System of English Laws in a neighbouring Province, establishing therein an Arbitrary government, and enlarging its Boundaries so as to render it at once an example and fit instrument for introducing the same absolute rule into these Colonies:

For taking away our Charters, abolishing our most valuable Laws, and altering fundamentally the Forms of our Governments:

For suspending our own Legislatures, and declaring themselves invested with power to legislate for us in all cases whatsoever.

He has abdicated Government here, by declaring us out of his Protection and waging War against us.

He has plundered our seas, ravaged our Coasts, burnt our towns, and destroyed the lives of our people.

He is at this time transporting large Armies of foreign Mercenaries to compleat the works of death, desolation and tyranny, already begun with circumstances of Cruelty & perfidy scarcely paralleled in the most barbarous ages, and totally unworthy the Head of a civilized nation.

He has constrained our fellow Citizens taken Captive on the high Seas to bear Arms against their Country, to become the executioners of their friends and Brethren, or to fall themselves by their Hands.

He has excited domestic insurrections amongst us, and has endeavoured to bring on the inhabitants of our frontiers, the merciless Indian Savages, whose known rule of warfare, is an undistinguished destruction of all ages, sexes and conditions.

In every stage of these Oppressions We have Petitioned for Redress in the most humble terms: Our repeated Petitions have been answered only by repeated injury. A Prince whose character is thus marked by every act which may define a Tyrant, is unfit to be the ruler of a free people.

Nor have We been wanting in attentions to our Brittish brethren. We have warned them from time to time of attempts by their legislature to extend an unwarrantable jurisdiction over us. We have reminded them of the circumstances of our emigration and settlement here. We have appealed to their native justice and magnanimity, and we have conjured them by the ties of our common kindred to disavow these usurpations, which, would inevitably interrupt our connections and correspondence. They too have been deaf to the voice of justice and of consanguinity. We must, therefore, acquiesce in the necessity, which denounces our Separation, and hold them, as we hold the rest of mankind, Enemies in War, in Peace Friends.

We, therefore, the Representatives of the united States of America, in General Congress, Assembled, appealing to the Supreme Judge of the world for the rectitude of our intentions, do, in the Name, and by Authority of the good People of these Colonies, solemnly publish and declare, That these United Colonies are, and of Right ought to be Free and Independent States; that they are Absolved from all Allegiance to the British Crown, and that all political connection between them and the State of Great Britain, is and ought to be totally dissolved; and that as Free and Independent States, they have full Power to levy War, conclude Peace, contract Alliances, establish Commerce, and to do all other Acts and Things which Independent States may of right do. And for the support of this

Declaration, with a firm reliance on the protection of divine Providence, we mutually pledge to each other our Lives, our Fortunes and our sacred Honor.

Does this sound familiar? The content of this document hits very close to home. Of course the grievances are for their times and situations, however it states and we will quote directly from within the actual content of the declaration, " That whenever any Form of Government becomes destructive of these ends, it is the Right of the People to alter or to abolish it, and to institute new Government, laying its foundation on such principles and organizing its powers in such form, as to them shall seem most likely to effect their Safety and Happiness. Prudence, indeed, will dictate that Governments long established should not be changed for light and transient causes; and accordingly all experience hath shewn, that mankind are more disposed to suffer, while evils are sufferable, than to right themselves by abolishing the forms to which they are accustomed. But when a long train of abuses and usurpations, pursuing invariably the same Object evinces a design to reduce them under absolute Despotism, it is their right, it is their duty, to throw off such Government, and to provide new Guards for their future security.--Such has been the patient sufferance of these Colonies; and such is now the necessity which constrains them to alter their former Systems of Government."

To put it in our terms, once again we are there,at a point in which we need to take the reins and make the modifications necessary for the "Safety and Well-being" of our people. So therein sets the premise of this dissertation. It's time…but how do we resurrect the old republic?

Chapter Two – Why a Republic

Considering the differences between a monarchy and a republic, why is one preferred over the other? In pre-medieval times the monarchy was preferred over a republic for reasons that made sense at the time. We must consider the time in which this history happened. The major movement at the time was Christianity. The prevailing idea was that of deific rule, where everyone was taught that everything was the result of God the Father. This caused a mindset of one ruler who was revered as a father sent by God to lead the public in the way that God instructed him to do.

As we now know, this had a horrendous effect on the people of the time. It was one of the worst times in the history of the world for people's rights. This is when slavery was the "modus operandi". There was much misuse of the populous. People were "owned" by their monarchs. The monarchy was organized like a large family in which the monarch was the father and all the people within his government were his children. This absolute subjugation was strictly enforced. People were punished (tortured) for simple misdemeanors such as eating too much of the monarchs crops in order to stay alive. The system of the time was the idea that everything was owned by the monarch. This system was such that the monarch would raise armies (from within his subjects) to conquer neighboring lands to impress the new conquered population into more subjugated family members whom would add to the coffers of the monarch (which is still going on today). These massive abuses in a relatively short time caused the people to see the futility of living this way and they became rebellious and inevitably changes were made. Hence we see revolutions en masse.

Not all monarchs were "bad", some were benevolent and fatherly. These could see that the way to get what they perceived as theirs was to treat their subjects with some kindness. They would provide ways for the rank and file to have a secure life, raise their families and thus breed more subjects for the monarchy. These monarchs were respected and even loved by their subjects. They were the reason much of medieval Europe stayed in this system for as long as it did. However, eventually, like all the governments before them, due to the inevitable temptation for abuse, nearly all fell.

Are you starting to understand how these systems are working? In my opinion and many others too, these systems, no matter how they were formed, eventually decayed and died. So a person should take from this situation that the death of our government is inevitable. However there is a way to avoid death. Maybe not for a human (at least until now) to live indefinitely, but theoretically, it is possible for an organization to extend its useful life.

At this point it may be interesting to note that each governmental system seems to last approximately 200 years then for some reason change happens. One theory is that when the system is formed in the beginning it was formed for good and ethical ideals, formed by using the theories of Aristotle or other philosophers like him, then the system would struggle and grow and become better and more efficient and productive, finally as it matures it becomes polluted with mistakes that were made during the life of the system. These mistakes, at least the ones that weren't corrected, begin to breakdown the internal workings and the overall system becomes untenable. This seems to be consistent with both political and economic systems. Both of these systems work in concert, when one is dysfunctional so is the other. (We will look at this phenomenon again.)

Understanding this concept of change, we as free citizens, must be aware of the workings of this phenomenon and embrace the idea of change. Throughout history our social order has been in constant flux. In ancient and medieval times the individuals didn't perceive the changes, as they didn't have the information of their changes at their disposal, but now with our access to information and technology, we are able to see so much more clearly. We are aware of the changes in social order happening worldwide right before our eyes, in nearly real time. Our concern now is to make the change that moves us in the correct direction, one that is in the proper evolutionary direction to provide us with the best safety and prosperity for us and our children.

Keeping in mind the historical concepts we have looked at previously, let's take a critical look at what has happen so far with our government.

In the beginning the **Founding Fathers** of the United States were the political leaders who signed the Declaration of Independence in 1776; some who took part in the

American Revolution and winning American independence from Great Britain; some who participated in framing and adopting the United States Constitution in 1787-1788 and some who put the new government under the Constitution into effect. Within the large group known as the "Founding Fathers", there are two key subsets: the "Signers of the Declaration of Independence" (who signed the Declaration of Independence in 1776) and the "Framers of the Constitution" (who were delegates to the Federal Convention and took part in framing or drafting the proposed Constitution of the United States). Most historians define the "Founding Fathers" to mean a larger group, including not only the Signers and the Framers but also all those who, whether as politicians, jurists, statesmen, soldiers, diplomats or ordinary citizens, took part in winning American independence and creating the United States of America. American historian Richard B. Morris, in his 1973 book *Seven Who Shaped Our Destiny: The Founding Fathers as Revolutionaries,* identified the following seven figures as the key Founding Fathers: Benjamin Franklin, George Washington, John Adams, Thomas Jefferson, John Jay, James Madison, and Alexander Hamilton.

In the winter and spring of 1786-1787, twelve of the thirteen states chose a total of 74 delegates to attend what we now know as the Federal Convention in Philadelphia. Nineteen delegates chose not to accept election or attend the debates; for example, Patrick Henry of Virginia thought that state politics was far more interesting and important than national politics, though during the ratification controversy of 1787-1788 he claimed, "I smelled a rat." Rhode Island did not send delegates, because of its politicians' suspicions of the Convention delegates' motivations. Of the 55 who did attend at some point, no more than 38 delegates showed up at one time.

These delegates represented a cross-section of 18th century American leadership. Almost all of them were well-educated men of means who were leaders in their communities. Many were also prominent in national affairs. Virtually every one had taken part in the American Revolution; at least 29 had served in the Continental Army, most of them in positions of command. Scholars have examined the collective biography of them as well as the signers of the Declaration and the Constitution.

Political experience

The framers of the Constitution had extensive political experience. By 1787, four-fifths (41 individuals), were or had been members of the Continental Congress. Nearly all of the 55 delegates had experience in colonial and state government, and the majority had held county and/or local offices.

- Thomas Mifflin and Nathaniel Gorham had served as President of the Continental Congress.
- The ones who lacked congressional experience were Bassett, Blair, Brearly, Broom, Davie, Dayton, Alexander Martin, Luther Martin, Mason, McClurg, Paterson, Charles Pinckney, Strong, Washington and Yates.
- Eight men (Clymer, Franklin, Gerry, Robert Morris, Read, Sherman, Wilson, and Wythe) had signed the Declaration of Independence.
- Six (Carroll, Dickinson, Gerry, Governor Morris, Robert Morris, and Sherman) had affixed their signatures to the Articles of Confederation.
- Two, Sherman and Robert Morris, underwrote all three of the nation's basic documents.

- Dickinson, Franklin, Langdon, and Rutledge had been governors.

The 1787 delegates practiced a wide range of high and middle-status occupations, and many pursued more than one career simultaneously. They did not differ dramatically from the Loyalists, except they were generally younger and less senior in their professions. Thirty-five were lawyers or had benefited from legal education, though not all of them relied on the profession for a livelihood. Some had also become judges.

- At the time of the convention, 13 men were merchants: Blount, Broom, Clymer, Dayton, Fitzsimons, Shields, Gilman, Gorham, Langdon, Robert Morris, Pierce, Sherman, and Wilson.
- Six were major land speculators: Blount, Dayton, Fitzsimons, Gorham, Robert Morris, and Wilson.
- Eleven speculated in securities on a large scale: Bedford, Blair, Clymer, Dayton, Fitzsimons, Franklin, King, Langdon, Robert Morris, Charles Cotesworth Pinckney, and Sherman.
- Twelve owned or managed slave-operated plantations or large farms: Bassett, Blair, Blount, Butler, Carroll, Jenifer, Jefferson, Mason, Charles Pinckney, Charles Cotesworth Pinckney, Rutledge, Spaight, and Washington. Madison also owned slaves, as did Franklin, who later freed his slaves and was a key founder of the Pennsylvania Anti-slavery Society. Alexanger Hamilton was opposed to slavery and, with John Jay and other anti-slavery advocates, helped to found the first African free school in New York City. Jay helped to found the New York Manumission Society and, when he was governor of New York in 1798, signed into law the state statute ending slavery as of 1821.
- Broom and Few were small farmers.

- Eight of the men received a substantial part of their income from public office: Baldwin, Blair, Brearly, Gilman, Livingston, Madison, and Rutledge.
- Three had retired from active economic endeavors: Franklin, McHenry, and Mifflin.
- Franklin and Williamson were scientists, in addition to their other activities.
- McClurg, McHenry, and Williamson were physicians, and Johnson was a college president. (Excerpted from Wikipedia.)

Taking this historical account as the actual events that transpired, the original United States was technically organized as an Oligarchy. In that the government was not organized and developed by the entire populous, but by a select few influential men who were charged by the people to organize a system of politics and economics that would work most efficiently for the times and the people for whom it was designed.. Some of the key points to look at are; the diversity of the Congressional Convention. The make-up was not, as our government has become, fraught with professional politicians as it is today. In fact, today the vast majority of our federal positions are currently filled with either Lawyers or Political Scientists (lawyers). It was, instead, very diverse. Bits and smatterings of a myriad of professions, Farmers, land speculators, men who speculated in securities, physicians, retired persons, even a college president. Yes, there were lawyers and people experienced in government, but the bottom line is that a wide cross-section of our people was represented when the country was formed, that gave the Continental Congress the best information about what was needed and what was not needed for the government to operate in the most efficient manner for the majority of the population at the time. Even though the beginning was organized as an Oligarchy, it was so diverse the majority of the populous was amply represented consequently the original Constitution was crafted with sufficient input from the populous to represent the majority of the people's needs. Is that still the case?

So in the beginning we based our operating system on what we had learned from Aristotle and Cicero, it looks like our "Founding Fathers" were on the right track. Pretty good start. So what has transpired since? To attempt to figure out what has happened let's look at our original Constitution and see what it contains and maybe why it was written the way it was.

First - The Declaration of Independence –

The Declaration justified the independence of the United States by listing colonial grievances against King George, and by asserting certain natural rights, including a right to revolution. Having served its original purpose in announcing independence, the text of the Declaration **was** initially ignored after the American Revolution. This Declaration was originally drafted as a resolution to the Virginia house of Burgesses in 1772 to bring redress to the government of Great Britton. The Declaration was circulated around the colonies to be ratified. Its stature grew over the years, particularly the second sentence, a sweeping statement of individual human rights:

Paragraph One:

When in the Course of human events, it becomes necessary for one people to dissolve the political bands which have connected them with another, and to assume among the powers of the earth, the separate and equal station to which the Laws of Nature and of Nature's God entitle them, a decent respect to the opinions of mankind requires that they should declare the causes which impel them to the separation.

This is the section that gives the justification for redress. With this paragraph we set the standard that if at any time we recognize such causes that would give us the opinion that there are abuses against the populous of this nation then we, as a nation must effect a change.

Paragraph Two:

We hold these truths to be self-evident, that all men are created equal, that they are endowed by their Creator with certain unalienable Rights, that among these are Life, Liberty, and the pursuit of Happiness.

This sentence is probably the most recognizable sentence in the English language. It personifies the ideals of both Aristotle and Cicero. It's almost taken word for word from Aristotle's work "Politics". Let's take a quick look at the entire text to see if this document has any credence at this time.

*We hold these truths to be self-evident, that all men are created equal, that they are endowed by their Creator with certain unalienable Rights, that among these are Life, Liberty and the pursuit of Happiness. That to secure these rights, Governments are instituted among Men, deriving their just powers from the consent of the governed, **That whenever any Form of Government becomes destructive of these ends, it is the Right of the People to alter or to abolish it, and to institute new Government, laying its foundation on such principles and organizing its powers in such form, as to them shall seem most likely to effect their Safety and Happiness**.*(This is the part that needs redressing today. Our present Government has become ineffective to providing the "governed" meaning the people of these United States with the rights to pursue Life, Liberty, and the pursuit of Happiness.) *Prudence, indeed, will dictate that Governments long established should not be changed for light and transient causes; and accordingly all experience hath shewn, that mankind are more disposed to suffer, while evils are sufferable, than to right themselves by abolishing the forms to which they are accustomed. But when a long train of abuses and usurpations, pursuing invariably the same Object evinces a design to reduce them under absolute Despotism, it is their right, it is their duty, to throw off such Government, and to provide new Guards for their future security.*

We hold these truths to be self-evident, that all men are created equal, that they are endowed by their Creator with certain unalienable Rights, that among these are Life, Liberty and the pursuit of Happiness.

Let's take this phrase first, as it is indeed first in the Declaration of Independence. Once again this sentiment harkens back to the writings of Aristotle… ", the city-state is composed of individual citizens, who, along with natural resources, are the "material" or "equipment" out of which the city-state is fashioned." These "natural resources" to which Aristotle alludes are in fact the natural resources of the people, the basic needs they require to have a rich life, freedom to do what is required to live comfortably and pursue their dreams, I. E. Life, Liberty and the Pursuit of Happiness. This is setting the basic premise of the Constitution. This initial paragraph is setting the foundation upon which the Constitution was developed.

Paragraph Three

(Redressing of the grievances)
Such has been the patient sufferance of these Colonies; and such is now the necessity which constrains them to alter their former Systems of Government. The history of the present King of Great Britain is a history of repeated injuries and usurpations, all having in direct object the establishment of an absolute Tyranny over these States. To prove this, let Facts be submitted to a candid world.

If this is read in modern context and we inject the word of States instead of Colonies and the office of president instead of King, it reads as many people feel today.

Let's address these reasons for changing the government one at a time;

He has refused his Assent to Laws, the most wholesome and necessary for the public good.

Laws are presently being promulgated over which we have no control. These laws are being perpetrated upon us at the whim of the current Congress and President. We have no say so as to the applicability or necessity.

He has forbidden his Governors to pass Laws of immediate and pressing importance, unless suspended in their operation till his Assent should be obtained; and when so suspended, he has utterly neglected to attend to them.

Example: Arizona

He has refused to pass other Laws for the accommodation of large districts of people, unless those people would relinquish the right of Representation in the Legislature, a right inestimable to them and formidable to tyrants only.

We have "representation", but to what ends?

He has called together legislative bodies at places unusual, uncomfortable, and distant from the depository of their public Records, for the sole purpose of fatiguing them into compliance with his measures.
He has dissolved Representative Houses repeatedly, for opposing with manly firmness his invasions on the rights of the people.

He cannot dissolve Representative Houses, but he (the President) opposes with firmness any suggestion that is against his agenda.

He has refused for a long time, after such dissolutions, to cause others to be elected; whereby the Legislative powers, incapable of Annihilation, have returned to the People at large for their exercise; the State remaining in the mean-time exposed to all the dangers of invasion from without, and convulsions within.
This is still being done through political appointments and will continue until we the people change the way government operates..

> *He has endeavoured to prevent the population of these States; for that purpose obstructing the Laws for Naturalization of Foreigners; refusing to pass others to encourage their migrations hither, and raising the conditions of new Appropriations of Lands.*

Hence our government pushes to legalize illegal immigrants by usurping the prevailing laws.

He has obstructed the Administration of Justice, by refusing his Assent to Laws for establishing Judiciary powers.

A case can be made in this area as to the manipulation of the Supreme Court, but it's minor and we can address it later.

He has made Judges dependent on his Will alone, for the tenure of their offices, and the amount and payment of their salaries.

The President and the Supreme Court.

He has erected a multitude of New Offices, and sent hither swarms of Officers to harrass [sic] our people, and eat out their substance.

Let me count the ways…Social Security, HAS, DEA, Education, Energy, Etc..

He has kept among us, in times of peace, Standing Armies without the Consent of our legislatures.
Yeah, one that is not applicable…so far
.

He has affected to render the Military independent of and superior to the Civil power.

He has combined with others to subject us to a jurisdiction foreign to our constitution, and unacknowledged by our laws; giving his Assent to their Acts of pretended Legislation:

For Quartering large bodies of armed troops among us:

For protecting them, by a mock Trial, from punishment for any Murders which they should commit on the Inhabitants of these States:

For cutting off our Trade with all parts of the world:

For imposing Taxes on us without our Consent:

Yes!!

For depriving us in many cases, of the benefits of Trial by Jury:

For transporting us beyond Seas to be tried for pretended offences

For abolishing the free System of English Laws in a neighboring Province, establishing therein an Arbitrary government, and enlarging its Boundaries so as to render it at once an example and fit instrument for introducing the same absolute rule into these Colonies:

For taking away our Charters, abolishing our most valuable Laws, and altering fundamentally the Forms of our Governments:

For suspending our own Legislatures, and declaring themselves invested with power to legislate for us in all cases whatsoever.

Granted he hasn't tried to suspend our Legislature, but he does invest himself with the power to legislate over us without any input from the people whatsoever.

He has abdicated Government here, by declaring us out of his Protection and waging War against us.
He has plundered our seas, ravaged our Coasts, burnt our towns, and destroyed the lives of our people.
He is at this time transporting large Armies of Foreign Mercenaries to compleat the works of death, desolation and tyranny, already begun with circumstances of Cruelty & perfidy scarcely paralleled in the most barbarous ages, and totally unworthy the Head of a civilized nation.
He has constrained our fellow Citizens taken Captive on the high Seas to bear Arms against their Country, to become the executioners of their friends and Brethren, or to fall themselves by their Hands.
He has excited domestic insurrections amongst us, and has endeavoured to bring on the inhabitants of our frontiers, the merciless Indian Savages, whose known rule of warfare, is an undistinguished destruction of all ages, sexes and conditions.
In every stage of these Oppressions we have Petitioned for Redress in the most humble terms: Our repeated Petitions have been answered only by repeated injury. A Prince whose character is thus marked by every act which may define a Tyrant, is unfit to be the ruler of a free people.

This last paragraph has happened repeatedly and we just experience the same distasteful result...more of the same. We can't, in any way that I know, communicate effectively with any member of the federal government. Albeit, they get so many communications they seem overwhelmed by our communication. Isn't that because we are discontent? If they were discharging their jobs with alacrity and zeal, responding to the will of the majority of the people to provide a government that was seeing to the premise that the ideal government would be providing the needed machinations so as to keep the populous happy and free, then we wouldn't be "communicating" to them as frequently.

So with this many of the same redresses occurring again and again, it would seem the Declaration of Independence has become, once again, applicable. This time, however, it seems these changes can be made in another way. War is not the preferred mode of change because we would have to harm our fellow citizens, some of whom are not involved in the crimes of the system . What I recommend is reorganization and rebirth. We can rebuild to a more modern method of operating, using the original documents as our guide, an historical document that is fraught with wisdom and insight and update it with more wisdom and insight to make it better and more applicable to these days and times. Even build in or maintain the provision for periodic change when change becomes necessary again.

Without belaboring the point, most of us are aware of the myriad problems within the Federal Government. The largest and most noticeable being the handling of our Economy and its own budgetary process. This is the main factor that will bring about the demise of the United States as we know it if something isn't done immediately!

Our System is on the brink of total collapse! We cannot sustain this free spending and wholesale printing of money any longer. As powerful as our economy was once, now it is only a memory of what it once was. We still harbor dreams of how great we were, but taken in the light of day we realize we are no longer occupying that position. Can we get it back? Yes, if we do our due diligence our economy can be re-energized to its former glory. Therein rests the motivation for this book. What we need as a nation is to develop a plan for the rejuvenation of our Federal Government and our National Economy.

We have looked at the Declaration of Independence, now let's peruse the Constitution itself and see what is applicable and worth keeping. Before we begin let me say this…Our Founding Fathers were wise and learned. They were guided by circumstances and possibly other forces to craft a document that has governed us for these 235 years and the majority of this time has been well met. Now we need to revisit this august document with a critical eye as to its applicability and sustainability for these days and times.

The Constitution of the United States of America

First it is the supreme Law of the United States. The Constitution is the framework for the organization of the United States government and for the relationship of the federal government with the states, citizens, and all people within the United States. This is key to our examination of the document. Being the framework of the federal government it needs to be closely examined as to its current applicability. My examination has uncovered areas that can and, in my opinion, should be modified.

The Constitution creates the three branches of the national government: a legislature, the Bicameral Congress (House of Representatives and the Senate); an executive branch led by the President; and a judicial branch headed by the Supreme Court. The Constitution specifies the powers and duties of each branch. The Constitution reserves all powers not specifically enumerated within the document to the respective states and the people, thereby establishing the federal system of government. This is another major point of scrutiny. I.E. What is appropriate now and what needs updating.

The Constitution was adopted on September 17, 1787, by the Constitutional Convention in Philadelphia, Pennsylvania, and ratified by conventions in each state in the name of "The People". The Constitution has been amended twenty-seven times; the first ten amendments are known as the Bill of Rights. Here is a big area of contention. Many of these amendments are out dated and should be removed from the document. Remember the Constitution was first written as a basic plan on which to manage the federal government. It was built in such a way as to limit the amount of power the federal government had over the people and it was actually a document to give the people the absolute power as opposed to the feds. We, the people, were supposed to manage our government's machinations not the other way around. Not like it is today. It seems anything you want to do, you must first check to see if it's OK with the feds! How did that happen? Answer…through the maturing and polluting of the federal governing process.

Explaining the Constitution.

Aristotle stated:
The city-state (i. e. our federal government) is a hylomorphic (i.e., matter-form or another way of thinking of it could be body and soul) compound of a particular population (i.e., citizen-body, this is us) in a given territory

(material cause, the United States) and a constitution (formal cause). The constitution itself is fashioned by the lawgiver and is governed by politicians, who are like craftsmen (efficient cause), and the constitution defines the aim of the city-state (final cause.)

Cicero stated:

The commonwealth was the property of the people, who entrusted it to the magistrates to be used for the common good, and that the "welfare of the people is the supreme law

So when it comes to this, when the government no longer fills the happiness needs of the population what do we do? Then it's time for a Constitutional Convention. Up until now we haven't need one, but to see how our government operates I think it's about time to relook at our system.

Chapter 3- The Inevitable Death of the Federal Government

Now we're beginning to see how our government has entered into a phase of self-degradation. The system has become corrupt from years of unscrupulous public figures abusing the federal governance by passing laws and attaching pork or earmarks to bills that has nothing to do with the original intent of the bill the pork is just a way of getting that person's personal agenda attached to the bill for their own personal greed. The federal government also, through normal operation, has committed errors in judgment by the well-meaning politicians passing bills which looked good in the short term but proved to be detrimental for the long haul. What has happened is the government "aristocrats" have developed a myriad of bad habits because they **assumed** the United States' productivity was omnipotent. Our cash generating machine was so robust they, as crooked politicians and as well-meaning ones, could sneak through any form of "legal" stealing and the people would simply pay for it with no ramifications to them. This is what happened with our Social Security System. Because the social security fund was so large the politicians thought they could "borrow" from the fund and not have to worry about the money ever running out. Of course if you ask them they will tell you they had always intended to put the money back into the fund, but something else always came up to divert their attention on to another emergency. Well look at where we are now. I am not privy to how much needless spending has been perpetrated on the people over the years, but if we decide our money must be used more responsibly, then this is one area over which we must have more control. We cannot give these spend thrifts the purse strings of our economy and allow them to continue to spend us into oblivion. They will always give a perfectly rational explanation of how we need the spending they want to cast upon us and it's for our own good. We just don't understand how important it is to have this new bill and so on and so on...

Let's take a look at some examples of how this system has worked throughout the short history of our country. Reams of examples could be written here as there are so many, but we will only look at a couple to exemplify the situation. How about Prohibition? That was good. We really needed that one. Actually we still have people today that think we should not drink. They will argue the evils of the demon rum, and prove their case eloquently and in full truth. They are absolutely right. Abuse of alcohol is a dastardly thing and some people should stay away from drinking is it tends to ruin people who misuse it. So just because some goody-two shoes decides through her truthful justification that it's bad for you, we should amend the Constitution and make it illegal for everyone? Well, that's what they did! They didn't try to see if there was a country-wide sentiment that Prohibition was best for the entire country, no, they just figured it was good to change the entire character of the United States.

How this came about:

Prohibition in the United States, also known as **The Noble Experiment**, was the period from 1919 to 1933, during which the sale, manufacture, and transportation of alcohol were banned nationally as mandated in the Eighteenth Amendment to the United States Constitution.

The United States Senate proposed the Eighteenth Amendment on December 18, 1917. Having been approved by 36 states, the 18th Amendment was ratified on January 16, 1919 and effected on January 17, 1920. Some state legislatures had already enacted statewide prohibition prior to the ratification of the 18th Amendment.

The "Volstead Act", the popular name for the National Prohibition Act, passed through Congress over President Woodrow Wilson's veto on October 28, 1919, and established the legal definition of intoxicating liquor, as well as penalties for producing it. Though the Volstead Act prohibited the sale of alcohol, the federal government did little to enforce it. By 1925, in New York City alone, there were anywhere from 30,000 to 100,000 speakeasy clubs.

While Prohibition was successful in reducing the amount of liquor consumed, it stimulated the proliferation of rampant underground, organized and widespread criminal activity. Prohibition became increasingly unpopular during the Great Depression, especially in large cities. The bulk of America became disenchanted after the St. Valentine's Day Massacre in 1929. Until then, they felt that, even with setbacks, Prohibition was working.

On March 22, 1933, President Franklin Roosevelt signed into law an amendment to the Volstead Act known as the Cullen-Harrison Act, allowing the manufacture and sale of certain kinds of alcoholic beverages. On December 5, 1933, the ratification of the Twenty-first Amendment repealed the Eighteenth Amendment. However, United States federal law still prohibits the manufacture of distilled spirits without meeting numerous licensing requirements that make it impractical to produce spirits for personal beverage use.

This type of slow development of deprivation is one of the sure signs that we are in the final stages of organizational death. These clues are something Adam Smith wrote about in his book "Wealth of Nations". He theorized about the growing of social and economic populations from villages to towns to cities to countries and eventually to a world government. As bad as those theories are for our nation there are also many good observations stated in this work One of the best for our style of growth is the theory of free enterprise. His theory was that unfettered business activity was good for the economy. This is true, however, even with this theory too much of a good thing can have bad results as well. The failing economy we are experiencing now is, in addition to our federal government, the product of mega-monster corporations who control our commodities and services so as to remove any competition in the markets. Another bad thing we learn from Adam Smith is how he explained the growth of governments. The bigger the government, the more of the economy they consume. The more of the economy consumed by government the less GDP (gross national product) left for the growth of business. Using only that theory we can see where our economy is headed.

The prohibition, or "dry", movement began in the 1840s, spearheaded by pietistic religious denominations, especially the Methodists. The late 19th century saw the temperance movement broaden its focus from abstinence to all behavior and institutions related to alcohol consumption. Preachers such as Reverend Mark A. Matthews linked liquor-dispensing saloons with prostitution.

Some successes were registered in the 1850s, including Maine's total ban on the manufacture and sale of liquor, adopted in 1851. However, the ban in Maine was repealed in 1856. The movement soon lost strength, and was marginalized during the American Civil War (1861–1865).

The issue was revived by the Prohibition Party, founded in 1869, and the Woman's Christian Temperance Union, founded in 1873. Despite its name, the latter group did not promote moderation or temperance but rather prohibition of alcohol. One of its methods to achieve that goal was education. It was believed that if it could "get to the children" it could create a "dry" sentiment leading to prohibition. (Supporters of prohibition were nicknamed "Dry"; opponents were called "Wet".)

In 1881, Kansas became the first state to outlaw alcoholic beverages in its Constitution, with Carrie Nation gaining notoriety for enforcing the provision herself by walking into saloons, scolding customers, and using her hatchet to destroy bottles of liquor. Nation recruited ladies as the Carry Nation Prohibition Group, which Nation also led. Other activists enforced the cause by entering saloons, singing, praying, and urging saloon keepers to stop selling alcohol. Many other states, especially in the South, also enacted prohibition, along with many individual counties.

In the Progressive Era (1890–1920), hostility to saloons and their political influence became widespread, with the Anti-Saloon League superseding the Prohibition Party and the Woman's Christian Temperance Union as the most influential advocate of prohibition.

Prohibition was an important force in state and local politics from the 1840s through the 1930s. The political forces involved were ethno-religious in character, as demonstrated by numerous historical studies. Prohibition was demanded by the "dries" — primarily pietistic Protestant denominations, especially the Methodists, Northern Baptists, Southern Baptists, Presbyterians, Disciples of Christ, Congregationalists, Quakers and Scandinavian Lutherans. They identified saloons as politically corrupt and drinking as a personal sin. They were opposed by the "wets" — primarily liturgical Protestants (Episcopalians, German Lutherans) and Roman Catholics, who denounced the idea that the government should define morality. Even in the wet stronghold of New York City there was an active prohibition movement, led by Norwegian church groups and African-American labor activists who believed that Prohibition would benefit workers, especially African-Americans. Tea merchants and soda fountain manufacturers generally supported Prohibition, thinking a ban on alcohol would increase sales of their products

In the 1916 presidential election, both Democratic incumbent Woodrow Wilson and Republican candidate Charles Evans Hughes ignored the Prohibition issue, as was the case with both parties' political platforms. Democrats and Republicans had strong wet and dry factions, and the election was expected to be close, with neither candidate wanting to alienate any part of his political base.

In January 1917, the 65th Congress convened, in which the dries outnumbered the wets by 140 to 64 in the Democratic Party and 138 to 62 among Republicans. With America's declaration of war against Germany in April, German-Americans—a major force against prohibition—were widely discredited and their protests subsequently ignored. In addition, a new justification for prohibition arose: prohibiting the production of alcoholic beverages would allow more resources—especially the grain that would otherwise be used to make alcohol—to be devoted to the war effort. While "war prohibition" was a spark for the movement, by the time Prohibition was enacted, the war was over

A resolution calling for an amendment to accomplish nationwide Prohibition was introduced in Congress and passed by both houses in December 1917. By January 16, 1919, the Amendment had been ratified by thirty-six of the forty-eight states. On October 28, 1919, the amendment was implemented by the Volstead Act. Prohibition began on January 17, 1920, when the Eighteenth Amendment went into effect. A total of 1,520 Federal Prohibition agents (police) were given the task of enforcing the law.

Although it was highly controversial, Prohibition was widely supported by diverse groups. Progressives believed it would improve society as generally did women, southerners, those living in rural areas and African-Americans. There were a few exceptions such as the Woman's Organization for Prohibition Reform who fought against it. Will Rogers often joked about the southern pro-prohibitionists: "The South is dry and will vote dry. That is, everybody sober enough to stagger to the polls." Supporters of the Amendment soon became quite confident that it would not be repealed, to the point that one of its creators, Senator Morris Sheppard, joked that "there is as much chance of repealing the Eighteenth Amendment as there is for a humming-bird to fly to the planet Mars with the Washington Monument tied to its tail."

Many social problems have been attributed to the Prohibition era. Mafia groups limited their activities to gambling and theft until 1920, when organized bootlegging manifested in response to the effect of Prohibition. A profitable, often violent, black market for alcohol flourished. Powerful gangs corrupted law enforcement agencies, leading to racketeering. Stronger liquor surged in popularity because its potency made it more profitable to smuggle.

To prevent bootleggers from using industrial ethyl alcohol to produce illegal beverages, the government ordered the poisoning of industrial alcohols. In response, bootleggers hired chemists who successfully renatured the alcohol to make it drinkable. As a response, the Treasury Department required manufacturers to add more deadly poisons, including the particularly deadly methyl alcohol. New York City medical examiners prominently opposed these policies because of the danger to human life. As many as 10,000 people died from drinking denatured alcohol before Prohibition ended.

Making alcohol at home was very common during Prohibition. Stores sold grape concentrate with warning labels that listed the steps that should be avoided to prevent the juice from fermenting into wine. Home-distilled hard liquor was referred to as "bathtub gin" in northern cities, and moonshine in the rural areas of North Carolina, South Carolina, Georgia and Tennessee. Since selling privately distilled alcohol was illegal and bypassed taxation by the government, the law relentlessly pursued manufacturers. In response, the bootleggers in southern states started creating their own souped-up, stock-looking cars by enhancing their cars' engines and suspensions to create a faster vehicle. Having a faster vehicle during Prohibition, they presumed, would improve their chances of outrunning and escaping agents of the Bureau of Alcohol, Tobacco and Firearms (BATF), commonly called "revenue agents' or "revenuers". These cars became known as "moonshine runners" or "shine runners".

The cost of enforcing Prohibition was high, and the lack of tax revenues on alcohol (some $500 million annually nationwide) affected government coffers.

When repeal of Prohibition occurred in 1933, organized crime lost nearly all of its black market alcohol profits in most states (states still had the right to enforce their own laws concerning alcohol consumption) because of competition with low-priced alcohol sales at legal liquor stores.

Prohibition had a notable effect on the alcohol brewing industry in the United States. When Prohibition ended, only half the breweries that previously existed reopened. The post-Prohibition period saw the introduction of the American lager style of beer, which dominates today. Wine historians also note Prohibition destroyed what was a fledgling wine industry in the United States. Productive wine quality grape vines were replaced by lower quality vines growing thicker skinned grapes that could be more easily transported. Much of the institutional knowledge was also lost as winemakers either emigrated to other wine producing countries or left the business altogether.

At the end of Prohibition, some supporters openly admitted its failure. A quote from a letter, written in 1932 by wealthy industrialist John D. Rockefeller, Jr. states:

"When Prohibition was introduced, I hoped that it would be widely supported by public opinion and the day would soon come when the evil effects of alcohol would be recognized. I have slowly and reluctantly come to believe that this has not been the result. Instead, drinking has generally increased; the speakeasy has replaced the saloon; a vast army of lawbreakers has appeared; many of our best citizens have openly ignored Prohibition; respect for the law has been greatly lessened; and crime has increased to a level never seen before."

Some historians have commented that the alcohol industry accepted stronger regulation of alcohol in the decades after repeal, as a way to reduce the chance that Prohibition would return.

So there you have it, an abject social experiment put upon the American people for their own good by a select group of Social Reformers that failed miserably and in my opinion brought on the Great Depression. Was alcohol prohibition the main cause of the depression? No, but it was a huge factor.

There were multiple causes for the first downturn in 1929. These include the structural weaknesses and specific events that turned it into a major depression and the manner in which the downturn spread from country to country. In relation to the 1929 downturn, historians emphasize structural factors like massive bank failures and the stock market crash. In contrast, economists point to monetary factors such as actions by the US Federal Reserve that contracted the money supply, as well as Britain's decision to return to the Gold Standard at pre-World War I parities (US$4.86:£1).

As an example of how we feel about our federal government today a reprint of a joke that is being circulated around the internet is as follows;

How the Federal Government works

Once upon a time the government had a huge scrap yard in the middle of a desert. Congress said, "Someone may steal from it at night." So they created a night watchman position and hired a person for the job.

Then Congress said, "How does the watchman do his job without instruction?" So they created a planning department and hired two people, one person to write the instructions and one person to do time studies.

Then Congress said, "How will we know the night watchman is doing the tasks correctly?" So they created a Quality Control department and hired two people, one to do the studies and one to write the reports.

Then Congress said, "How are these people going to get paid?" So they created two positions, a time keeper and a payroll clerk, then hired two people.

Then Congress said, "Who will be accountable for all of these people?"

So they created an administrative section and hired three people, an Administrative Manager, an Assistant Administrative Manager, and a Legal Secretary.

Then Congress said, "We have had this command in operation for one year, and we are $918,000 over budget. We must cut back." So they laid-off the night watchman.

NOW slowly, let that sink in.

Quietly, we go like sheep to the slaughter.

 Does anybody remember the reason given for the establishment of the DEPARTMENT OF ENERGY.... during the Carter Administration?

Anybody?
Anything?
No?
Didn't think so!
Bottom line: We've spent several hundred billion dollars in support of an agency...the reason for which not one person who reads this can remember!

Ready?? It was very simple . . . and, at the time, everybody thought it very appropriate.

The Department of Energy was instituted on 8/04/1977 TO LESSEN OUR DEPENDENCE ON FOREIGN OIL. Hey, pretty efficient, huh???

AND, NOW, IT'S 2012 -- 35 YEARS LATER -- AND THE BUDGET FOR THIS "NECESSARY" DEPARTMENT IS AT A WOPPING $24.2 BILLION A YEAR. IT HAS 16,000 FEDERAL EMPLOYEES AND APPROXIMATELY 100,000 CONTRACT EMPLOYEES, AND LOOK AT THE JOB IT HAS DONE! THIS IS WHERE YOU SLAP YOUR FOREHEAD AND SAY, "WHAT WERE THEY THINKING?"

A little over 35 years ago, 30% of our oil consumption was foreign imports. Today 70% + of our oil consumption is foreign imports. Ah, yes -- the good old Federal bureaucracy!! They still have yet to OK the building of a pipeline to bring Alaskan oil to our refineries. That's efficiency!

NOW, WE HAVE TURNED THE BANKING SYSTEM, HEALTH CARE, AND THE AUTO INDUSTRY OVER TO THE SAME GOVERNMENT?

Hello!! Anybody Home?

We could go on and on with the various "mistakes" brought on by the federal government, World War II, Social Security, the IRS, etc., but that would take several more volumes and it wouldn't serve our purpose. I challenge you to name one federal program that has been successful. Suffice to say the feds have distilled themselves to the point of "professional politicians" who are now operating as a governmental social club. The "club" is so sought after by young politicians they will spend millions of dollars to belong. This club is not a new phenomenon. It has existed throughout history and it happens with regularity. This phenomenon occurs in all organizations that survive for a long time. We can call it "organizational aging".

This same phenomenon happens in all organisms both living and legally concocted. The same process occurs in business too. The major difference is in business a cure has been developed.

If the system is so dysfunctional, what do we do? If we do nothing else we should at least look at what was done throughout history and try to ferret out what worked and see if we can adapt that process.

In chapter 1, we looked at the theories of Aristotle, let's take another look at his theories and see if they would apply to our circumstances. Aristotle stated, the city-state (i. e. our federal government) is a hylomorphic (i.e., matter-form or another way of thinking of it could be to call it the body and soul) compound of a particular population (i.e., citizen-body, this is us) in a given territory (material cause, the United States) and a constitution (formal cause). The constitution itself is fashioned by the lawgiver and is governed by politicians, who are like craftsmen (efficient cause), and the constitution **defines** the aim of the city-state (final cause.)

So as we reason it out...Keeping in mind Aristotle is talking about a "City-State". When we use his analogy to liken our federal government to his theories we are committing a theoretical mistake. What he is discussing is a working theory within his form of governance during his lifetime, and what he says is true for the governmental situation at the time. They were organized within City-States. Being these City-States, they were small concentrations of people the government could efficiently operate within and be more responsive to the needs of the population, specifically because the government was dealing with a smaller number of people and could function better because of the smaller numbers, react to the people's needs quicker and more effectively (heck, in those days if the government had a question they would call in and interview individuals). Thinking of that theory we can see for our situation and using Aristotle's theoretical direction for the federal government, it should be the body and soul compound or entity of the people or citizens in the United States using our ratified Constitution and this Constitution should be governed by the politicians who are charged with leading this government efficiently as well as **frugally** to the people's final desires. That cannot happen. The infrastructure of our people is too large, too diverse and too dispersed for a government to presume it can make laws to cover all the situations for everyone. That is a physical impossibility. In order for us to have the government described by Aristotle and the type of governance we want, that being as much freedom as is possible, we need to reorganize our system of government to replicate the "City-State" of Aristotle.

So I would assume if this definition is being complied with we don't need to proceed any further. However, the question is…is this happening? From what I have seen…NO! So, what parts of this definition of Aristotle's are not in compliance? Let's look at each part of the theory and see if we can ascertain what is lacking and if it is lacking…why.

The first thing that jumps out to my scrutiny is in the first statement. According to Aristotle, the government should be the "body and soul" of the people. Through critical thought I would understand that to mean the government would be aware of our wants and needs and react to those needs in a comprehensive way so as to meet the needs of the **majority** of the citizens while being attuned to the freedoms of all and negotiating the best possible situation in which the populous can function. The only way to create this "body and soul" form of government is to organize it in such a way so as to respond quickly to the needs of the local population. A local government who can listen to and react to the changing needs of its local populous.

The next situation which needs attention within the Aristotle definition is the fact the government is not being run efficiently or effectively by "craftsmen" and it's not, in any way, fulfilling the people's final desire's or needs. In fact, it appears, by all intents and purposes, to be the antithesis of fulfilling any of the people's needs or wants, the government now seems to be passing legislation to satisfy their personal agendas or ways to stop people (passing more laws)from living their life in comfort and happiness.

So the idea that the politicians should be craftsmen is not applicable to our Congressmen. They are instead, at least it seems to me, professional thieves. They go to school for the express purpose of becoming a professional politician. Why would a person go to school to study Politics but to become a Congressman or governmental manager. Craftsmen are not "Professionals" they are highly trained artisans, people who intern for years to become adept at their craft and their craft does not have to necessarily have to be politics. One of the major imperfections in our Congress is that we do, in fact, have too many professional politicians, these politicians have no experience in any other subjects in which people may have needs. They are passing laws on transportation, medicine, public safety, education, etc. All these Congressional Professionals of today know is how to draft a bill. They are all, nearly to a person, Lawyers.

If we look at the example our founding fathers gave us, you will see the first Congress and several subsequent Congresses were comprised of a variety of Statesmen. We had Doctors, farmers, shop owners, merchants, ship owners, financiers, scientists and even a college president. This situation was set up using the ideas of Aristotle, those ideas being named *politeia* which consisted of a mixture of the other forms he argued this was one of the ideal forms of government. Polybius expanded on many of these ideas, again focusing on the idea of **diverse** government. Well, we no longer have "diverse government", what we have is a government of sameness. Even when we look at the supposed different ideologies of the Democrat and the Republican parties, there is no differences. What we have is a smoke screen expertly crafted to make us believe "our" philosophy is contained within the philosophies of the party of our affiliation and that that party in which we put our trust and support will react to and change government in a way which will give us happiness, security and freedom to do the things that make this country great. Really? (As they say on Sports Center,) Come on man! That myth can't be believed by anyone after experiencing the disasters our government has laid upon us in recent years. Both parties are identical. They both get up in Congress and work the same and if by some rare chance they get elected and go up to congress and really do want to do some good for the people, that ideal is soon changed by the "old school" senior congressmen who explain the "ropes" of how things are done in the federal government. Sooner or later the junior becomes indistinguishable from the senior.

The problem is, we were spot on when we started the government, and as time progressed the federal government, as all entities do, matured. With the passage of time the federal government began to change. The changes were insidious. It may have been only one nondescript Representative sneaked in and no one even noticed. The problems he caused were so miniscule it wasn't even worrisome enough to notice. Then another and another of these thieves soon got together and started plotting and planning how to put riders on bills to benefit themselves, as their numbers mounted they started gaining power. They then started making deals behind closed doors to help each other. Soon the majority of congress jumped on the bandwagon, as the greed mounted they all learned how to rape the public's money without anyone being the wiser. Now what do we have? A perverse self-perpetuating money grabbing monster that must be stopped or it will succeed in bringing about the ruin of our system. So it seems, taking all these observations into critical examination, keeping everything local and small seems to work well for both the governmental system and the economy as well. Let me ask you this, why are nearly all of the Congressmen Millionaires? If I were interested in becoming rich and powerful why would I want to do it by entering into politics? Again, according to the ancients, a politico should be a dedicated servant of the people. A person who cares about his constituency and is up there in Washington for the sole purpose of helping his people stay happy and free. Is that what they do today?

Therefore, using our powers of critical thinking, it would be obvious our present form of federal government isn't working as efficiently as we would hope it would. So, the only logical conclusion is that we need to change the way the federal government does it business.

What do we do? We can't just start changing our way of doing things willy-nilly. Oh, let's see…what can we do, this doesn't work so let's change it. Then we make some minute change and wait to see of it will work. Then if that didn't work we change something again and wait to see if that was any better. No, we need a process whereby we can use known methodology, things that are tried and true and implement those to effect the changes. Then when things change we make can continue to make the needed changes slowly and carefully so as not to adversely impact the population. Let's take a look at an area of our society where this process works well and has been working well for years…Business.

How does business, at least the successful ones, stay profitable? They do it by watching the moves being made in the business community. In which direction is the competition moving? Why? Should we move the same way or would another way be better for us? These few questions aren't all encompassing, not by any stretch of the imagination. It's a very complex process that we have neither time nor space to go into, but we do have another implement we can use to effectively explain the process we can use to help us reach our decision about how government should run.

It's called the "Organization's Life Cycle". This theory is what most successful long lived businesses use to gauge and effect changes within their economy. Here's how it works: The first stage is naturally called the "Start-up" phase. During this phase is when 95% of the businesses fail. This is as it should be. There are many reasons why a business will fail and those failures happen most often in the beginning. Finances are the biggest cause of failure, just not enough operating capital to keep the business running until it can begin to make a profit. Maybe the product is behind or ahead of its time (no customers). It could be the person who is beginning the business doesn't have the proper training to understand what is needed to make the business successful. Whatever the reason, and there are many more, this is when most businesses fail. This first phase can go on for years. The business can have ups and downs along the way, but if it survives, sooner or later, it begins to grow rapidly even exponentially.

This is phase 2, "Momentum". This is where the business has proven itself and is becoming profitable. This is the time when rapid expansion takes place, the entity is unfettered and exuberant, numbers of customers are growing and there is relatively little competition. During this phase is where business development is at its fastest, expansion in products and services happen rapidly at this level. Soon we get to a size where the business is of a comfortable size. It is functioning at its most efficient and further growth is slow and steady.

This is where we enter into stage 3 "Maturity". In maturity we become complacent, the business is operating well and profits are high. Everything is moving along smoothly and prosperously. This is also where we start to become lazy and if we are not careful we can begin allowing problems and inefficiencies to creep in, the business is able to absorb some inefficiency so it's not very noticeable. This is also where mistakes are made and some of those mistakes sometimes can become habits. When the entity reaches this point, it gradually enters into the final stage.

This is Stage 4. "Degradation or Death" stage. This is where competition has progressed and this business has been passed by. Businesses within the company's market has become more efficient and has grabbed much of the company's customers. This business has been prosperous in the past, it doesn't try to improve on its product line or methodologies. This can happen for any number of reasons, but if this entity continues on its present course it will inevitably end up in bankruptcy or at the very least with a severely diminished customer base and eventually close its doors. (Ever hear of layoffs? This is when they happen.)

That's the organizational life cycle in a nutshell. Not a definitive dissertation on the subject, but enough for us to see the workings of the process and get a feeling about how it will equate to the workings within our current federal government. You may have noticed the organizational life cycle seems to mirror the human life cycle almost exactly, except for one glaring fact that has not yet been mentioned. That fact is that the organizational life cycle, if handled correctly, can be perpetual.

Yes, you read that right. The system can be handled in such a way as to be a living entity forever. Constantly renewing itself and maintaining a dynamic organization that responds well to changes and keeps updating itself as needed to keep up with the changing times. Wouldn't it be nice to be able to install an operating system into our government that would cause it to be able to operate effectively and efficiently forever?

That is exactly what my proposition is…to design a system of governance in such a way as to be responsive to the needs and wants of the populous and be able to reinvent itself so as to remain effective and efficient forever.

Can this be accomplished? I think it can with wisdom, effective guidance and critical thinking. What we will do is first, understand the problem. Not just react to our feelings about what's happening now but think through the present situation and determine what is actually happening, whether the occurrence we are analyzing is worth considering or will it just be solved through another method. In other words not everything that arises needs to be fixed. If we try to fix everything that happens we will never be doing anything productive we will only be reacting to daily occurrences. One of the major points here is that we immediately see the federal government doesn't necessarily need to be in Washington 24/7. They can get their job done in a few weeks a year. So why not use the state representatives and have them meet in Washington those few times a year to meet the obligations of the Feds?

Chapter 4   How Do We Start

We have seen the system is broken, but what can we do? Where do we start so we can make some sense out of where the government is now and where we want it to be when we have met our goal.

We can start by looking at redundancy. What do we have in the structure of the United States governing system that is repetitive (and each costs money, by the way)? What I mean is, we are paying our government to provide us with services and guidance at different levels of government, why would we want to pay for the same service twice? To give you an example, would you go to a store like Publix with your list of needed groceries and buy those groceries for say $200. Then go over to Walmart and buy the SAME groceries again for another $200? NO!!

That's exactly what our government does…constantly. We pay for our services over and over and over and sometimes over again! Let's take just one example and we will move on. Our Police Force, if I remember correctly we have a City police force, a County police force, a State police force, a Federal police force, and an International police force. Could we manage to wedge in another police force in there somewhere. We shouldn't say that too loud because the feds will find a way to put in another one. I.E. Homeland Security? What in the hell do they do that our other 6 police departments can't?

Is there something I'm missing or is a criminal a criminal. What is the difference when a criminal breaks a law? Is there some special difference between a City criminal and a Federal criminal? Not that I can see…they all look pretty much alike. What about you? Can you tell me the difference between a federal criminal and a city criminal? What the lawyers are going to tell you is that the criminals have committed different levels of crime. So what? Are the insides of the court house any different other than the feds spend a lot more of our money on their elaborate edifices to show us how strong they are. The answer is NO! There is no difference between the federal level or the City level, both criminals are tried in a court of law. The only difference is the lawyers and the judges. They are supposedly professionals in the specialty. Actually the way I see it, they are a good ole boy network that works together to bilk us out of as much money as they can so they don't have to do any real work. Our judiciary system is so corrupt it would be my next challenge to fix after the federal government gets straightened out.

Seeing that we seem to have some redundancy in our governmental system, let's see if we can pare down some of the myriad departments within our government that are really NOT necessary but the politicians say they are.

Actually, you don't want to go through all the departments and discuss the pluses and minuses of each and every department agency and division. We will, as a litmus test take on a few of the obvious perpetrators, but suffice to say, if it's covered anywhere in lower governmental departments, agencies, or divisions it needs to go. I think I have mentioned this before, but it's worth repeating. Governing a population is best accomplished as close to the individual as possible! Governing lower down is better.

Now, let's take a look at a few departments just for fun. One of my favorites is the Department of Education. Now there's an important department. Exactly what is it they do? I'm not really sure but the bureaucrats tell us they monitor our national educational system so the states properly run their systems. In order to ensure the states comply, the feds hold on to the educational dollars dolling out the sweet parts to the states who best do what the feds want them to do or no money for you you've been a bad state! Take a look at their record. Since they have had control of the state's systems we have gone from one of the best educational systems in the world to the level of a second level system. So is it working? Why do we give the educational budget to the feds anyway? What are they going to do with it that the states can't do themselves except spend it on a lot of unnecessary people who don't contribute anything to the enrichment of our children.

To further enhance this example I will do another reprint from the Department of Education's Website. It says the following:

(Reprint from ed.gov)
all levels for school year 2009-2010, a substantial majority will come from State, local, and private sources. This is especially true at the **Education is primarily a State and local responsibility in the United States.** It is States and communities, as well as public and private organizations of all kinds, that establish schools and colleges, develop

curricula, and determine requirements for enrollment and graduation. The structure of education finance in America reflects this predominant State and local role. Of an estimated $1.1 trillion being spent nationwide on education at elementary and secondary level, where about 89.5 percent of the funds will come from non-Federal sources.

That means the Federal contribution to elementary and secondary education is at about 10.5 percent, which includes funds not only from the Department of Education (ED) but also from other Federal agencies, such as the Department of Health and Human Services Head Start program and the Department of Agriculture's School Lunch program.

Although ED's share of total education funding in the U.S. is relatively small, ED works hard to get a big bang for its taxpayer-provided bucks by targeting its funds where they can do the most good. This targeting reflects the historical development of the Federal role in education as a kind of "emergency response system," a means of filling gaps in State and local support for education when critical national needs arise.

(Are you getting this propaganda? "Targeting its funds where they can do the most good," really? What about all the thousands of salaries that are paid to the departments over 4000 employees? For what?) And it continues:

Mission

Despite the growth of the Federal role in education, the Department never strayed far from what would become its official mission: to promote student achievement and preparation for global competitiveness by fostering educational excellence and ensuring equal access.

The Department carries out its mission in two major ways. First, the Secretary and the Department play a leadership role in the ongoing national dialogue over how to improve the results of our education system for all students. This involves such activities as raising national and community awareness of the education challenges confronting the Nation, disseminating the latest discoveries on what works in teaching and learning, and helping communities work out solutions to difficult educational issues.

Second, the Department pursues its twin goals of access and excellence through the administration of programs that cover every area of education and range from preschool education through postdoctoral research. For more information on the Department's programs see the President's FY 2011 Budget Request for Education.

President's FY 2011 Budget is seeking $50.7 billion in discretionary appropriations for the Department of Education, an increase of $4.5 billion over the comparable discretionary total provided in the 2010 appropriations act.
The total increase includes up to $1 billion the Administration would request in a budget amendment only if Congress completes an ESEA

Reauthorization that includes the President's proposed reforms. (Why do we need an increase over last year, what has changed and who does he think he is? The last time I checked he didn't have any background in Education, if we look at Obama's experience it is in law. So how is he going to come up with proposals to reform our school systems? According to what I read in the budget they intend to spend $100 Billion on the implementation of their grand plan.

How do they have a $50.7 billion budget and then spend $100 billion? Can you explain that to me?)

So this is Obama's grand plan for our educational system. My question is, how is the federal government making the education of our children any better? In their own words, "The Department carries out its mission in two major ways. First, the Secretary and the Department play a leadership role in the ongoing national dialogue over how to improve the results of our education system for all students. This involves such activities as raising national and community awareness of the education challenges confronting the Nation, disseminating the latest discoveries on what works in teaching and learning, and helping communities work out solutions to difficult educational issues. How does that make our children any smarter? Also how does the National Government suppose that they know more about how local educational systems should work? All they do is try to make a system that is supposed to work for all locations, not for what would work for your child.

Second, the Department pursues its twin goals of access and excellence through the administration of programs that cover every area of education and range from preschool education through postdoctoral research." Administration does not make the quality of our education any better, they are only doing the same thing they just mentioned. They are sitting around having meetings talking about how great their programs are and how to spend more money at the federal level and not giving anything to our kids' school systems to help those systems put out a quality product to our kids.

Firstly, why do we need a Secretary and Department to lead…lead what? Our schools have a leadership system in place at the lowest possible level which as I think we all agree is the best form of leadership. All I see this additional leadership level doing is handcuffing local leaders and reducing innovation and creativity. This is the old maxim of rule with an Iron hand, which has never ended well, plus being supremely redundant and it reduces the freedom of the locals.

Secondly, what is meant by its twin goals of access and excellence through the administration of programs? I'll tell you what that means, that means the programs they concoct to develop their agenda, whatever that agenda may be. It's to manipulate and "manage our system to their own needs and political goals. Is this what our kids need? In other words if the locals don't knuckle under to what the regime wants they don't get their money and the kids suffer. Before the Department of Education was formed we were ranked #1 in the world. Where are we now?

In an article written by Christine Lagorio released by the AP September 13th 2005, states:

(AP) The United States is losing ground in education, as peers across the globe zoom by with bigger gains in student achievement and school graduations, a study shows.

Among adults age 25 to 34, the U.S. is ninth among industrialized nations in the share of its population that has at least a high school degree. In the same age group, the United States ranks seventh, with Belgium, in the share of people who hold a college degree.

By both measures, the United States was first in the world as recently as 20 years ago, said Barry McGaw, director of education for the Paris-based Organization of Cooperation and Development. The 30-nation organization develops the yearly rankings as a way for countries to evaluate their education systems and determine whether to change their policies.

McGaw said that the United States remains atop the "knowledge economy," one that uses information to produce economic benefits. But, he said, "education's contribution to that economy is weakening, and you ought to be worrying."

The report bases its conclusions about achievement mainly on international test scores released last December. They show that compared with their peers in Europe, Asia and elsewhere, 15-year-olds in the United States are below average in applying math skills to real-life tasks.

Top performers included Finland, Korea, the Netherlands, Japan, Canada and Belgium.

Given what the United States spends on education, its relatively low student achievement through high school shows its school system is "clearly inefficient," McGaw said.

Note: This is being put out by our own media. This was back six years ago, where are we now?

I could go on and on, but I think you get the idea. If you want to read the entire federal education budget go to www.ed.gov. It's all there in their own words. They think it's progressive and sage. Well it's not, what it is actually, is a program to dumb down our children and to reprogram them to the type of thinking that our government is our salvation and we should give them all of our money and let them take care of us from cradle to grave (the classic socialist ideal). What a great way to think. They do such a great job, think for a moment…can you give me an example of a federal government program that has actually worked?

That's only one department. I haven't even begun to enumerate all the special agencies, administrations and offices the feds have conjured up to usurp more of our money.

Here are just a few;

IRS, Homeland Security, FDA, EPA, CIA, FBI, Department of Commerce, Bureau of Farms, ACF, Administration for Toxic Substances and Disease Registry, USDA, African Development Foundation, Animal and Plant Health and Inspection Service, FAA, SEC, ATF, Bureau of Indian Affairs, **Bureau of Public Debt,** (What about the Bureau of Governmental Debt? Where's that one?) Bureau of Labor Statistics, **Bureau of Reclamation** (ever hear of this one? Maybe this is what we need to reclaim our federal government.) And the beat goes on…It covers literally the entire alphabet except X,Y and Z. If you would like to see the list personally google, 'departments of government' or 'www.usa.gov/Agencies/Federal/All_Agencies/index.shtml '. It will astound you. Always keep in mind we pay for all these offices and the people who operate them.

Suffice to say there is definitely some duplication within these hundreds maybe thousands of agencies, bureaus, departments etc. so it's my opinion we should eliminate the duplications. All of these offices need to be scrutinized as to their effectiveness and worth. If we can do without a particular office them we eliminate it. If an office is unique and not duplicated at the state, county or city level then we could keep it if and only if it proves to be efficient and viable. It needs to be understood that there are personal prejudices and preferences, so in order to make this plan work it will have to be put to the voters test. Would this be a huge program? Yes. Is it necessary for the government to be reorganized into an efficient governing body? Yes. So we will have to do what needs doing.

Herein lies the rub. All those agencies, bureaucracies, departments and offices that eat up gobs of our tax dollars are also employing millions of people. So when we fix the redundancy situation we will be putting millions of people on the street. We will cause an unemployment problem of monumental proportion. The best I can determine approximately 3.6 million work for the feds in some aspect. Of course not all will be laid-off, but most will. When we come to this point in the reorganization we will have to develop a program for the people who lose their positions. It will need to be a short term situation. The situation is we need to reorganize and unfortunately someone will lose their job.

The reason this needs doing is that without wading through the huge piles of budget bills we use to keep our obese monstrosity running, approximately 32.71% of the federal government is used to run these programs. That is a huge percent of the tax burden we must maintain as US citizens. Not only that, but why do we need such a large military? What better way can we handle Medicaid, Medicare and Social Security? Are there better ways to organize and run these huge drains on our money? I say let's take a look and see if we have alternatives. The bottom line is running the day to day operations of the Congress and the actual administration of our government is only about 5% of the total budget. Would that lessen our tax load a little?

Why does a farmer in Iowa have to pay part of his hard earned income to educate a child in Indiana, or a social security check for a geriatric in Massachusetts? Is it fair to have a Californian supplement the unemployed in Florida? The best answer for these and all other governmental situations is No. It's the responsibility of the people in their respective states to take care of their own. And for the populations in the respective states if you don't like the way your state does business then drag-up and move to a state that better fits your lifestyle. Today, it's not like it was back in Colonial times where the people congregated together to protect themselves from the big bad wolves or the scary sounds in the night. We are, or at least should be, mostly over that. If you don't like what you have now you can go out and use your plastic to get what you want.

Does our federal government have any job at all? Yes they do. It's the job for which they were originally contrived. They can take care of traffic between states, mitigate disagreements between states, handle international situations and provide for the defense of the nation. I'm over simplifying the situations as it will entail more complexity then I care to go into here, but that will be worked out when the deed is accomplished.

In a nutshell what I propose is to go back to the original Declaration of Independence and Constitution, and add one more amendment, the idea of that amendment being that all the previous amendments are null and void and that we start over. I realize this may not happen, as it will be the decision of the people of the United States who will decide the ultimate outcome of the reorganization of the federal government, but I can't help injecting my opinion, and I invite you to do the same. Contact me at http://www.resurrectingtherepublic.org

But that's not all I would recommend for the great reorganization. In my opinion we need to devise a way to mitigate the operations of the feds without having them devise a way to slowly and surreptitiously grab power back again. The challenge here is that wielding huge amounts of power have the effect on people of giving them the desire to have more. We would all like to be king for a day or so. Of course if you actually were king for a day the following day you would like to do it for another day and so on. This is a normal tendency. It's something that when we finally reorganize the fed we need to plan to avoid. The Monarchy is dead, long live the king.

We have to devise a system of governmental positions which will not have the ability to keep a given person in office so long as for them to become a fixture within the federal government. I am suggesting, for lack of a better idea at the present, strict term limits for any elected governmental officials. This length will have to be determined by whomever reorganizes the system. My first thought would be eight years. We want to avoid any cliques and secret societies from being formed within the congress. Fresh new blood every eight years would give new sets of eyes looking at the operations and new ways of looking at and doing things. We could look at other governments and the systems they use, however I would suggest we make sure the process at which we are looking has some semblance of efficiency. We are talking about our system of Congress, not the people who work within our government on a daily basis to keep the machine working. These normal workers should continue their jobs whatever they may be and however the job should last.

Another suggestion to be looked at will be a system where the elected state officials such as state senators and state representatives would be required to sit in the Federal Congress for determined times during the year to do the business of the Federal Congress. Now this suggestion to run the federal government from the states will undoubtedly raise some ire from many people who will say that due to the complexity of the world today that this form of government would be impossible. I say they may be right, however, we need to take a look at several different ways to do things, maybe we can come up with a viable system.

I'm not suggesting we go back to the eighteenth century and start over, I'm saying we have new and extremely powerful technology that can be properly used to create a government that would be more efficient and effective. We need to examine these possibilities and decide if they will be more responsive and intuitive towards creating a more peaceful and freer nation than we have now.

Why not avail ourselves of the new technology? Does it have pitfalls? Yes. Are there tendencies to abuse these systems? Absolutely. Those inadequacies have been around no matter what system has been tried in the past, so let's not obviate a tool without at least giving it a critical inspection to see if it has merit. With due diligence and careful planning the proper safeguards can and will be developed and implemented. The people of the United States would not be so naïve as to put the running of our federal government on Facebook.

With the power and creativity we possess in our software industry, we can develop the system that is needed to safeguard our governmental processes quite effectively. As a matter of fact, if we look carefully at what is needed for our government to operate effectively, we may find that all the so called security we have in our government today may not be as needed as we are led to believe. Thinking critically, what do we do in big time world government today that requires such hush-hush secrets? They will protest that foreign governments are constantly trying to usurp our secrets so as to somehow get one over on us. But what are they trying to steal? Our military secrets? Maybe, I'll give them the benefit of the doubt on that one, but what else? How much wheat we are going to sell to China? How the peace talks are going between Israel and the Palestinians? What? The only other situation that might be worthy of some secrecy would be the Presidents travel plans.

Really all the secret machinations going on today are mainly due to the propaganda prevalent with the corrupt bureaucratic monster that exists now. If the Congress was fully forthcoming with all their dealings there would be no need for secrecy. All they are supposed to be doing is handling international business and political dealings with other countries, not some sexy intrigue designed to get something over on some unsuspecting government or faction.

Are there requirements to help other countries in need…absolutely, after we have taken care of our house. In any family you take care of your situation first then help the neighbors. Our federal government should operate the same way. When I exercise my budget I pay my bills first then I give to charity a portion I have which is left over when the bills are paid. Does this make sense? You don't give money to the heart foundation until you have paid the bill on the family car.

Our federal government must operate in the same fashion. This is a good place to put a control point. Not only do we need a constitutional law controlling the use of the federal budget but I would suggest a computer program that exercises absolute oversight over any and all expenditures by the federal government. My justification for this type of program is that our current system has too many loop holes that enable the present senators and representatives too much leeway to spend, spend, spend. If they think an emergency has arisen then they pass some kind of new appropriation and print some more money to HELP with the new situation. Most of the time the situation can be resolved through other means, by the states, by a reexamination of the circumstances that caused the "emergency" in the first place, or letting time work it out.

Now are there times when the feds may need to act and use other monies to correct a situation? Yes. So what should they do? My solution would be to appeal to their bosses, the states. Bring the situation to the states, explaining the problems and the reasons why this situation must be addressed by the federal government and not by the states. Not only bring the problem, but also bring the solution and let the states decide if the condition requires needs to be handles with more money. If it does then the states can decide how much to provide for the correction of the circumstances. This way the budget remains balanced and the one-time expenditure is remedied. This form of reparation will cause a majority of the states to ratify the solution or the solution goes unsolved. This method will be a case of a "second and third and fourth" opinion and so on to carefully examine the problem and ensure the emergency is in fact an emergency and it truly needs fixing. Yes, there are times when a quicker action will need to be taken. These instances will have to be very carefully examined and strict controls on what those instances are and how they are addressed must be developed and instituted. AT NO TIME WILL WE LET THE CONGRESS HAVE THE POWER TO MANIPULATE THE STATES OR THE PEOPLE FOR ANY REASON. All these types of activities will be under the strictest control by the states and the people. I would go as far as to say this form of government could be likened to a reverse monarchy where the people have the absolute power over the government. This would be the highest form of governing at the lowest possible level.

So far in this chapter we have looked at and removed redundancy. This will have the effect of reducing federal government spending and allowing us to create under close scrutiny of the states the ability to keep a balanced federal budget, and making the federal congress tow the mark by keeping them under restrictive rules and laws. So what else would be advantageous to keep our states free and in total control?

Abolish all federal taxation. I have alluded to this many times, so now let's come clean. All financial control every single dollar will be under the scrutiny and control of the state governments…period. All financial requirements that may be required to run the feds will be managed by the state governing bodies. All control of the budget needed to run the federal government will be totally allotted by the states and the budget, which is developed two to three years in advance, will be submitted to the states for ratification and through the computer program which will be instituted for the control of these expenditures. A portion of this budget will be a surplus, a portion allotted to be used for contingencies and emergencies that can and will come up from time to time. This surplus will be maintained by the states in an escrow type of budget account that can't be used for extraordinary situations that may arise.

It is my opinion any entity must operate at a profit. The federal government is no different. They must operate at a profit to be able to execute ongoing programs which must be maintained. For example, government employees retirement programs, some systems that will be deemed under federal control because the system operates through several or all states like the FAA. I'm not here to say the FAA will continue to be a federal program, I'm only saying that there may be programs that will operate most efficiently under federal control. So the states will include these types of programs in federal control and provide the instruments necessary to run the programs. However, let me reiterate, all fiscal requirements of the federal government will be under control of the majority of the states, if there is a question about what money is needed or why...the answer will be settled by the states themselves not with any power passed down to the feds.

I would even go as far to suggest there may be a way to poll the people for their opinion as to what their feelings are about the required moves needed. My caveat on this form of control would be to ensure the system is as foolproof as possible and have a process that would guarantee the individual who was expressing their opinion was in fact the person they are represented to be. This could be very tricky, but with our technology and a lot of testing and scrutiny, I think a secure system of technology could be developed. Inevitably there will most likely be a small margin of error. What we would require would be a rule as to the amount of error that would be acceptable. I would strive for the least amount of error as possible. This would provide us with the highest amount of confidence that we were getting the most correct response of the people's opinion. Once we had that level of confidence, the states could more effectively respond to the people's requirements. Of course this type of program does not yet exist. The development of such a program will be extremely complex and difficult to pull off but it can be done, and when it is accomplished we will be closer than ever before to having a truly responsive government, one that will be attentive to the people's needs and be active and receptive in its operation.

We need to be able to control the activities of the federal government as though it was our teenage child…when a child is in its development years it thinks it knows what's good for them but we as parents have been there and done that so we know that the child need only listen and learn so they will mature and become wise in their activities. They can become a good child and be successful one day, but for now we need to handle them with strict control. Well, that's how we need to handle the federal government…with strict control and iron hand management. In other words don't give them the family credit card and let them run amuck with no oversight. Does that make sense?

Let's take a look at what I propose to change the Federal Government and reorganize it into the great and strong government it once was.

Chapter 5 – All Business has a Useful Life

Most of us can agree that our federal government system is broken. The case has been made through equating our current situation to historical observation and making recent examinations, through theory and actual fact. So what do we do? Is it so broken that we might as well find a rock and hide under it and watch as our whole government collapses around us? No…we still have time to right the sinking ship. It will take some hard choices and the healing process won't be pretty, in fact, most of us are going to have to hurt a lot in order to correct the corruption and inefficiencies rampant in the government today, but it will be worth it. Through diligence and wisdom, we can reorganize our federal government and regain our status in the world as the only super power on the planet. We can reestablish our stature to the level where we once were as the true leader of the world and push to even higher heights. If you are any kind of Red Blooded American then you want us to again be the leader of the world. Americans want to lead the world, it's what we do. We are winners and can't stand to lose. So how do we begin?

We can begin by accepting our present position. In our present condition, we are losers. We weren't losers in the past…we were winners, but we somehow through incessant and insidious degradation of our federal governmental system lost our leadership status and now, we're losers. Once we accept that premise and move on we can begin to fix the situation and get back to our winning ways. We are just like a formerly great athletic team. For example, let's say two years ago our team won the Super Bowl, and then through the actions of corrupt owners, our team loses all of its best players. What happened was the owners decided to trade off all the best players and siphon off the huge amounts of profits gained from not having to pay the large salaries of these star players. The owners advertise through propaganda in the media that they will rebuild the team for an even greater team. What they actually do is go out and get people who have less talent and play for less money. Not the good players who took us to and won the Super Bowl, but players the owners could pay less money and make a huge profit for a few years through all the ticket sales to the unsuspecting public who wanted to see our great team play. It works for a year or two, then everyone learns and they stop coming to watch a mediocre team who loses all the time. It's the same old story…money. Unscrupulous business people who will do anything to make another buck no matter what it takes. That's the old business theory that these sleaze bags perpetrate on the public. Actually it's not a business theory at all. It's a con man's theory, the type of business where all that matters is the bottom line. I'm here to tell you that it is not the correct way to run a business or especially not a way to run a government. This idea espouses the erroneous notion that it's everyone for themselves. The old rationalization that it's dog eat dog and the only way to be successful is to take everything you can, damn the other guy. Sorry, that idea is passé. If we have learned anything from history it's the fact that people are social entities and the best way to be better and grow our success is to work within our society to take care of each other. A very important point here is, the best way to be governed is by being lead from the lowest level. It's not, as our federal government tries to tell us, that one size fits all. That might be alright for socks, but not for people. People have unique needs depending on the area of the country and the people who are being governed. The more we work together at this lower level the better our society becomes and the stronger we are.

Business...good business strives to produce a product that gives value, service and quality. The business, which provides all these things while at the same time has ethical practices, is constantly improving its product, staying abreast of the competition and looking for newer and better products or services to provide its customers. You see, the idea of a good business is to add something to the community. When the business has done its thing the community in which it operates is better off because the business was there. That's the kind of theory and ethics we need to rebuild into our government. We require a government that when all is said and done leaves us better off for that government being part of our country. Does that make sense?

So how do we accomplish this radical change without completely destabilizing the world? It's not going to be easy. We need to move slowly and carefully. It's not as if we just purchased a fixer-upper house and we can go inside and start ripping down the walls and rebuilding it into a like new house for the next owner. We can't just rip everything apart and get out the spit and glue and start putting the pieces back together again, this is not Humpty Dumpty.

We are dealing with people's lives. Thousands, perhaps millions of people like you and I are getting their sustenance from this currently operating slum lord we call the Federal Government, we can't just decide to throw everyone out of their housing (like our present government would do). Because, no matter how bad it is right now, it still provides some form of protection for these unfortunate folks. We have to find another way. We need to develop a way whereby we can manage the reorganization in a more humane manner. Sure, we are going to fire or lay-off a lot of people, but we can manage this transition as an ethically organized plan to make the transition a bit easier. In other words we don't want to switch from one slum lord to another. That's the old way let's not get caught up in that modus operandi.

Let me propose a different theory, there is an axiom in business that states, "All business has a useful life which emulates human life". There is a birth, a period of growth, a maturing process, followed by old age (infirmity) and finally death. The term used by most business theorists is Organizational Life. So right now you are probably thinking...so what that's nothing new. If we were only talking about human life you would be exactly right, however, in the case of organizational life it is not precisely the same. The way organizational life developed was a bit unique from physical life. We use the same life development cycles, but we have the ability to prolong life indefinitely.

Here's how it works. Let's say we decide to go into a business, just for sake of explanation we will call it a widget business. Widgets are a good example as they don't exist and we don't have to have people telling us we are operating our business improperly. After all, this is only an example to be used for clarification.

We get together a nucleus of people, and in the beginning we recruit several experts in the manufacturing, operation and marketing of widgets. We are determined to put together the finest widget research money can produce. We have researched other widget manufacturers and are satisfied our product is the best on the market today. So with much excitement we begin.

Our first steps will be tenuous at best. In this start-up phase, we begin our process, but there are a million questions…are we adequately financed? Are our processes correct? Can we find enough customers to make us successful? And so on. So after we suffer through this tenuous time we emerge successful we have weathered the onslaught from the competition and we are ensconced in the business of building great widgets and have become a factor in the Widget industry.

Now, the next and most exciting stage…Exponential growth. If we survive the start-up stage and with our acceptance into the industry, gain a place to sell our product, we will enter into the stage called momentum. We attain our deserved reputation of quality and innovative approach of the widgets produced by our company and we are dominating the industry. Now we grow in leaps and bounds. We are enjoying huge amounts of profit and market growth. With our new found profitability we engage in a period of expansion. We build new plants and distribution centers all over the world. We are at the top of our game. So we are enjoying our success. We may even increase the salaries and benefits of the principals within the company. We may even over hire a few relatives to "take care" of our families. Of course they deserve their rewards; they stuck with us in the lean times.

We have become inarguably the top of our industry. The unchallenged behemoth of all widget companies in the world at this time. So we settle in and prepare to enjoy our well-deserved rewards for all our hard work, sweat and tears. This will continue for a period of time, a time where we will live on our laurels, so to speak. During this time we will continue to produce an acceptable amount of widgets and the quality will remain the same or, because of an influx of less than interested new company employees who may only be in the company to garner a great paycheck and may not be as interested in the quality of the product as we once were, the quality may deteriorate slightly, but we are still doing well. Profitability is there and we still have the majority of our loyal customer base, but for some reason we haven't been growing as fast lately. What's happened is the original crew, at least most of them, have moved on in one way or another and the replacements are not what you would call overly excited about producing great widgets they're more interested in getting the great money and benefits they are getting by having their position in the company. (This is called the maturity stage).

Then, out of the blue, appears a new bunch of young guns (A lot like we were years ago). A new group of engineers (perhaps some of our old employees)who have come together and developed a new digitized version of the widget, this product is not only better, faster and smaller than our conventional widget, but it's cheaper to make and it lasts longer. We are devastated. In a matter of weeks or maybe months we have lost our customer base, and our widget has gone the way of the buggy whip. We don't have anyone in the company who knows anything about digital processes and can't seem to find anyone who is willing to work with us until we can get up to speed. We finally realize that if we don't get up to speed on technology we will be forced to file for bankruptcy. So we see the demise of our illustrious widget company.

That is, as I'm sure you realized, the life cycle of a business (at least an example of one). The same life cycle happens to all entities, human, biological, business, and government. For the last two, however, it doesn't need to be that way. There are methodologies available that if used

Organizational Life Cycle

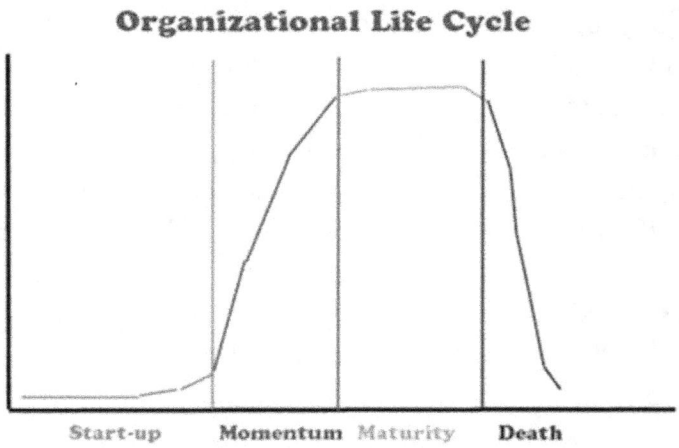

Start-up   Momentum Maturity   Death

expeditiously can breathe new life into the business or

government entity and that entity will be able to extend its life indefinitely. Next we will take a look at how we can accomplish this phenomenon.

The way it works is when the business has entered the final stage of life, that business must reinvent itself. Take IBM for example. It started out as a company that built and sold mechanical business machines.

An example of the perpetuation of Business
(Reprinted from Wikipedia - IBM historical archives)

Although IBM was incorporated in the state of New York on June 16, 1911 as the Computing- Tabulating-Recording Company (C-T-R), its origins can be traced back to developments at the close of the 19th century. For example, the first dial recorder was invented by Dr. Alexander Dey in 1888, and Dey's business became one of the building blocks of C-T-R. Similarly, the Bundy Manufacturing Company was incorporated in 1889 as the first time recording company in the world, and it, too, later became a key component of C-T-R.

When the diversified businesses of C-T-R proved difficult to manage, Flint turned for help to the former number two executive at the National Cash Register Company, Thomas J. Watson, Sr. In 1914, Watson, then age 40, joined the company as general manager.

The growth and extension of C-T-R's activities made the old name of the company too limited, and, on February 14, 1924, C-T-R's name was formally changed to International

Business Machines Corporation. By then, the company's business had expanded both geographically and functionally, including the completion of three manufacturing facilities in Europe.

(Here comes one of the first reorganizations that extend the business life of the company).

Just as his father saw the company's future in tabulators rather than scales and clocks, Thomas J. Watson, Jr., foresaw the role computers would play in business, and he led IBM's transformation from a medium-sized maker of tabulating equipment and typewriters into a computer industry leader.

Under Thomas J. Watson, Jr., there were also innovations in marketing. In 1969, IBM changed the way it sold technology. Rather than offer hardware, services and software exclusively in packages, marketers "unbundled" the components and offered them for sale individually. Unbundling gave birth to the multibillion-dollar software and services industries, of which IBM is today a world leader.

On April 7, 1964, IBM introduced the System/360, the first large "family" of computers to use interchangeable software and peripheral equipment. It was a bold departure from the monolithic, one-size-fits-all mainframe. Fortune magazine dubbed it "IBM's $5 billion gamble."

(Therefore a completely new life in business hence a new life cycle).

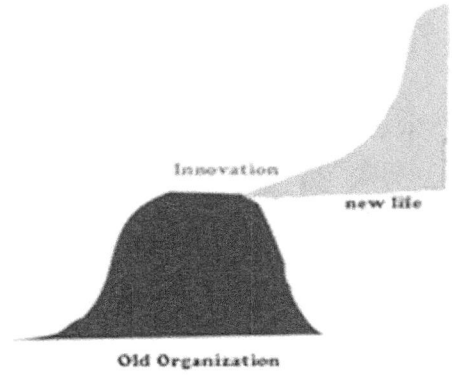

Most of us know the rest of the story. I don't know if IBM still leases "360's". Actually it doesn't matter. The fact remains the company has survived for one hundred twenty-three years and will continue to exist through innovation and reorganization.

So that's what I suggest for our governmental system. It's broken, so much so that it has become dysfunctional. In my eyes, it's time to innovate and reorganize. Let's face it, as a federal government our system is dying. If we don't reorganize we die. Which will you choose?

I could cover many other companies who achieved the same life extension, but it would be overkill. Suffice to say the Organizational life cycle is for real and the methods for life perpetuation… work.

The next question should be…will it work for the federal government? I say why not? The federal government is a "social business" entity and as such is obliged to follow the rules of business operation as is every other business in existence. Therefore it's my opinion we should treat the federal government the same way using the same rules and tools.

So that begs the question…which business rules do we invoke first? Remember we have members of our society currently working for and raising their families on the excesses of the federal government, possibly through no fault of their own. Not to mention the HUGE social system the government has amassed. You can't just stop the Social Security checks, Medicare and Medicaid payments or for that matter shut down the Welfare system, you must redress these malfunctions and slowly decrease these programs until they grow themselves out of existence.

Taking this into consideration we need to be aware of the chaos we can perpetrate upon our society if we just close down redundant services and do wholesale layoffs. Making a move such as this could throw our monetary and economic systems into turmoil. Without any control of this great country everything would be anarchy.

I feel a prudent path of reorganization would be to first organize a group who would be responsible for the total realignment of our federal government and give them an assignment to develop a comprehensive plan on how to update the feds so the government can operate more efficiently and effectively for our country. Not as the dysfunctional bureaucracy it is today, but more of what we need to function in today's technological world. This group would consist of a coalition of representatives from the individual states and be comprised of the exact number of Senators and Representatives there are presently in the Federal Congress. A side bar here would be that thinking about the rate of speed needed to acquire knowledge today as opposed to how quickly knowledge was amassed in past history…we may want to keep a system in place whereby we can keep abreast of the movement of the world's innovations so as to be attuned to keeping up with or even ahead of the rest of the world's political systems. In essence I am suggesting the possible organization of a new type of governance. I know that sounds counterproductive, we are trying to reduce the government and doing it by adding another branch, but hear me out. By organizing this new watchdog branch of government we can meliorate and mitigate the current government while making the changes we deem necessary. Not only will this new branch make the reorganization more orderly, but this group can oversee the machinations of the present congress to insure there is no backdoor intrigue or clandestine planning or subterfuge.

Reorganization Plan

My first recommendation is to stop the financial bleeding. The whole governmental process requires redress, but the main cause of most of our grief is budgetary overruns. Fix the bleeding first. It's my assessment we must pass a law to only spend what is allotted to spend and not a penny more. Is this going to cause upheaval in the ranks of government? Yes. What must be done must be done. I look at it this way, if I didn't have enough money to buy gas for the car until next payday, then I either wait to get paid or if I need gas to get to work, then I need to scrimp somewhere else in order to make it to payday. In my family we called that "robbing Peter to pay Paul". There are several ways to accomplish this, maybe we must take a pay cut for the rest of the year or take a few days off without pay or close the offices completely for a week or so. Are any of these measures so bad? We don't have to fire or lay-off anyone or if the offices are closed for a week can't you still get your business done, just done a week later. What is so wrong with that?

To my way of thinking this is the single most important move that must be made to get the system back on track and operating within the needed constraints. The people must take complete and total control of the dealings of government in order to start the process of reorganization. We all realize retrofitting the government is an extremely complex and difficult process, so many things are ensconced in our daily lives. things we may not even realize. We have hidden taxes, governmental fees, federal regulations, national restrictions. All these and a myriad of others must be handled.

Our first step and probably the most traumatic will be to stop the Congress from spending any more of our hard earned money. The coalition of states will take charge of dispensing the current budget. They will spend the money as needed and as they see fit. At the same time it is recommended the Congress be dissolved. We don't want them to think they can somehow sneak in and pass some sort of protectionist law to prevent the reorganization from happening. This is one area where there may be some bad feelings, due to the entire Congress being replaced by responsible people who aren't playing politics.

My assessment is to move on this reorganization slowly. If we try to make sweeping cuts and close departments without taking into consideration the ramifications of our actions we could decimate our way of life. We need to improve our plight, yes, but let's do it by causing the least amount of social upheaval. We need to keep in mind these government workers are citizens of this country. Here is a proposed methodology for the reorganization.

1. Take charge of the running of the government by having complete control of the budget.
2. Place a moratorium on law making until such time as the coalition deems the reorganization complete or events of an emergency nature occur. (Funds can be set aside for such events.)
3. Put together a consultant group (a coalition of all the states) for the assessment of the Constitution and all national laws.

4. Another group will be formed to study the effectiveness and legality of each federal department, I.E. Are they profitable, efficient and delineated in the Constitution? The group will then develop a plan for either the closing of the unit or the restructuring of that department, possibly disassembling it and apportioning the several parts to individual states for operation at the state level. Each department will be examined critically to see if there is any value to keeping the organization and reorganizing the unit into a profitable entity. (This includes offices, agencies and any other entity that is currently being run by the feds).

5. A plan will be developed to return states' rights and powers back to the states in an organized manner. This plan will be implemented by a separate commission which will be cooperating with the other two groups. All movement and reorganization will be fully disclosed by each group and all groups' moves and decisions will be fully disclosed to the citizens of the United States.

6. Another team will begin examining all federal programs. This team will work in concert with the Budget oversight committee. The programs that must be closed will be done so in a way so as to inflict minimum impact on the people who are currently operating these programs. We will need to move carefully on these phases. We need to evaluate the social impact and budgetary impact of each move.

Profit motive

As in business, each and every Federal entity will have to organize in such a way as to be profitable. For some reason we seem to have been taught the idea government cannot be profitable. I ask why not? If each area of the Fed was profitable then they could subsidize their own expenses such as payrolls, overhead and retirement plans. Albeit we would have to maintain a watchful eye on where the profit goes and how it can be spent, but I have always been a proponent of healthy competition so why can't the federal government compete with the rest of business and get into the business of making profit? I say they can. Again, the only caveat being the playing field must remain level. The feds would have no material advantage like changing the laws so they would have any monetary or legal advantage over any other business in their particular field accept the same ingenuity and innovation the rest of those businesses possess. As long as the competition stays fair and just, the process can only benefit everyone. This would be a great way to lower the tax burden on the people of the United States. The people who would pay for the running of a particular branch of the government would be the section of society who made use of those services.

One major implementation in my eyes is that any government within the United States, both federal and state level will not have the power to become a government run monopoly. Any organization having unrestricted freedom to do anything they deem necessary is a festering cesspool of temptation for corruption(example the IRS). Everything we do here in the US needs to be driven by competition. That way we will have the best chance to maintain a healthy environment.

Social Programs

In addressing the current social programs issue, both federally and state run, we need to work on eliminating these millstones from around our collective necks. My suggestion would be a two phased approach.

First, the development of an alternative program would need to be designed. Something whereby people nearing retirement or disabled would be able to live a dignified life for their remaining years, this will not be easy, it's going to take some of the brightest minds we have at our disposal. We are going to need a program that is self-funded. It cannot require any government subsidies or funding of any kind. It is a necessary program and will be developed by some clever people to take care of our elderly in the manner to which they have become accustom.

After that program is developed and implemented, we can then begin to phase out all the remaining social programs that are currently running within the federal and state governments. These should be phased out naturally by allowing the programs to end as they would normally. As the people who are currently on the systems leave the system through whatever means they do, then no more people will be enrolled. People who are new to the program would have an opportunity to switch to the new programs and not lose their accumulated benefits. This way all our seniors, indigents and disabled will be taken care of and the system can be retired with the minimum amount of consternation.

Chapter 6 - Machinations of the Resurrection

Let's take a look at what's happening in the world. The United Kingdom, Ireland, China, mostly Greece and other nations on the continent of Europe and the Middle East... Their economic and political challenges have arrived. We stand on the same doorstep. That is why we need to act now."

So how does this all happen? In this chapter we will discuss some possibilities, but keep in mind nothing is cast in stone. These thoughts are compiled by the research and critical thinking of only one person. That person is not all seeing nor is he a sage (at least I don't think so). The theories that will be proffered forth are only a beginning suggestion. The actual plan and implementation may require modification at various times as the situation changes. As other people enter into the equation and other facts are brought to light, things change and improvements can and most likely will happen. A major question here is, how will this program be funded? The answer is through contributions from concerned citizens. Not by ANY government monies. The rest will happen as it should through the will and needs of the people of the United States.

Amendment 10 - Powers of the States and People. Ratified 12/15/1791.
"The powers not delegated to the United States by the Constitution, nor prohibited by it to the States, are reserved to the States respectively, or to the people."

Note this well. Anything not expressly granted to the Federal government is reserved for the States and/or the People. Although this amendment is very liberally interpreted, it is one of the tenets of the Constitution. This amendment is also known as the States' Rights Amendment.

Keeping in mind the "Organizational Life Cycle" theory, we should realize the present governmental process is in its final stage of this process and demands reassessment. With this in mind, the several states that will form the Coalition will have to act to curtail the powers of the federal government. Here's the suggested plan:

The Initial Plan

After the organizing of the Coalition, a series of committees would be formed to assess the functionality of each department, division, agency or office within, controlled by or any part of the federal government, in other words every entity of the federal government. Everything they have anything to do with needs to be examined and after being scrutinized by a group or several groups, it must be determined through the criteria developed by the Coalition, if the entity is viable or not.

Our first step will be to organize the Coalition of states (which can be done legally under the 10th Amendment) to address the grievances these states have with and about the running of the federal government. The Coalition will be comprised of assignees from all the states within the Coalition. Once this Coalition is formed it will have to be controlled by an agenda. This agenda will be developed by a designated group of representatives formed by the original Coalition. The group or committee which will be formed will be an entirely independent group for the purpose of studying and reporting to the Coalition as to the requirements given to them by the Coalition. (The purpose of this is to keep diversity in the process) with only one group the tendency could be that they would develop some personal agenda. It is required we keep as much personal feeling out of this process as is possible to produce an environment that satisfies the majority of the population, not our personal likes and dislikes. The method of populating the committee could be accomplished in any number of ways, my recommendation would be to have the representatives be ordinary citizens selected from the populous, a select number of citizens from each state. Men and women, who have demonstrated a history of success, people who are a microcosm of the original Congressional committee, people from all walks of life. The more variation the better, this will bring to the table a diverse pattern of critical thinkers, which will have the tendency to spawn fresh ideas about how to accomplish the task before them. The bottom line on this process is diversity, I strongly recommend the persons who are selected to these committees be picked by the people of the state from which the committee comes by popular vote, not by the Governor, or the state legislature or any state agency. There is too much temptation to get a state's political agenda into the process and that could taint the workings of the process. This could be accomplished through a social website as a "Wiki" type of comment page about each issue. Depending on how viable the Coalition would feel about the security of the internet and social networking, it seems that using state of the art media to evaluate modern social change would, in my estimation, be apropos. I have set up a website...HTTP://www.resurrectingtherepublic.org. This could be used for the purpose.

With this simple statement is how we will affect the changes deemed necessary and just and we will proceed thusly.

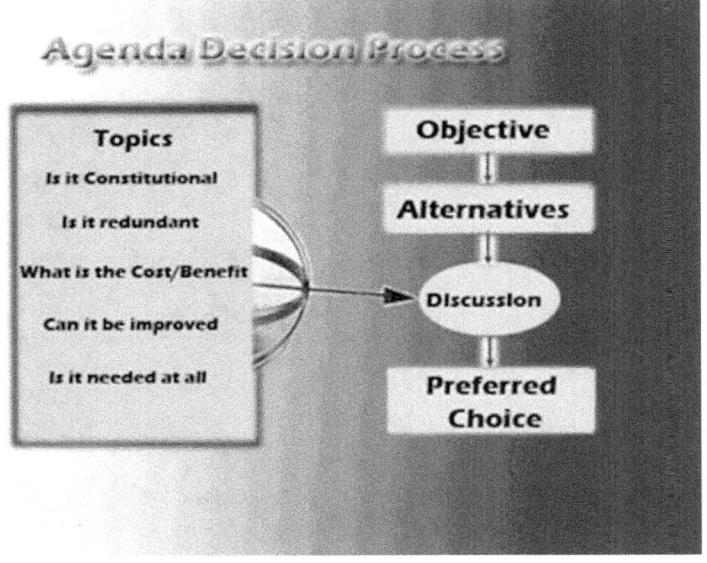

The suggested method will be for the "2nd Constitutional Convention" Committee to look at and determine if a given program is of any value to the governmental system.

First the Comittee will address the question is this unit (office, agency, committee etc.) Constitutional? If the response is no then the Coalition will develop an objective. Next they will make a list of alternatives. Once these alternatives are listed another discussion will ensue to prioritize and decide upon a preferred choice.

If the answer to the Constitutional question is yes it is Constitutional, then they would ask the next question...Is it redundant? If this question is yes, then the Coalition would go through the same steps as it did in the Constitutional query and the rest of the process follows the same steps through each of the queries for Cost/Benefit, Improvement or is it needed.

These decisions of the Committee are only a recommendation of the Committee. Each of these choices will need to be put through another decision making process.

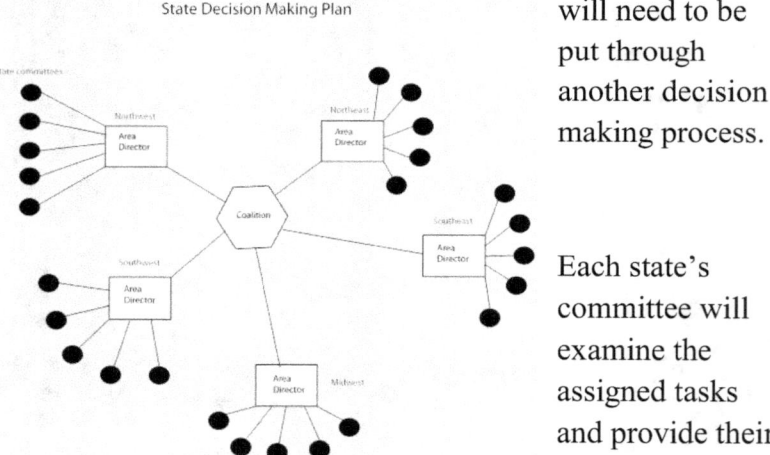

State Decision Making Plan

Each state's committee will examine the assigned tasks and provide their recommendations. The suggested decision making process is recommended so as to garner the most diverse recommendations: Each State will receive the following directions:

a. Receive the assignment
b. Initiate Committee analysis
c. Research using Agenda Decision Process (shown above)
d. Make a tentative recommendation
e. Test recommendation through computer analysis
f. Complete the recommendation for plan of implementation
g. Issue the recommendation to Area Director

Once the Area Director of the 2nd Constitutional Convention has the recommendations from all the State Committees, the 2nd Constitutional Convention Committee will then collate all the recommendations from those states and reissue these recommendations to the other states to reexamine the recommendations and ask for a second assessment. (This will give each state the opportunity to view the other states recommendations and see if there are other options that may be better than the ones they suggested. After completing the decision making process once more, the final recommendations will then be submitted to the Area Director and the 2nd Constitutional Convention Directors Committee who will decide on the final Area recommendation then send it to the Coalition for implementation. Through this process of redundancy the final outcome should be as close to the majority's decision as is practicable.

The 2nd Constitutional Convention Committee will review all the recommendations from all the Area Directors and using their recommendations, they would then formulate a decision in which direction to go. This can be done by National Vote or some other method decided by the 2nd Constitutional Convention Coalition (I recommend popular vote, but care will have to be taken to ensure honesty in the vote).

Once the direction is decided upon, the 2nd Constitutional Convention Committee will develop a plan for implementation of that decision. When the plan is completed it can be assigned to an action committee which will begin implementation. At this juncture an inspection system will be needed to insure the proper carrying out of the plan. The successful application of this plan could be done by instituting several decision points for monitoring the progress towards the goal. Each of these decisions points will create opportunistic places for inserting needed changes or reassessment of the plan if the development seems to be going astray.

Once this agenda is developed and delivered to the 2nd Constitutional Convention, the 2nd Constitutional Convention would examine the agenda and decide how to proceed with the implementation of the recommendations of the committee.

We need to keep in mind several things here. First is the original ethics of Aristotle, how the government should be driven so as to keep the people happy. Next to ensure we are complying with the Constitution and lastly adhering to our final requirement to run the government as we would if it were a profitable business. If we can achieve all these items then I think we will have gained our goal.

My last suggestion is that we need to be constantly aware that Organizational life cycle is a constantly moving system so it need to be watched and assessed and when necessary it should be addressed and changed when needed.

Chapter 7- What's the Fix

The Federal Budget and what needs to be cut.

Department of:	2012 Projected
Expenditures (in $ Billions)	
Agriculture	23.9
Commerce	8.8
Defense	553
Education	77.4
Energy	29.5
Health and Human Services	79.9
Homeland Security	43.2
Housing and Urban Development	48
Interior	12
Justice	28.2
Labor	12.8
State and other International Programs	47
Transportation	13.4
Treasury	14
Veterans Affairs	61.85
(End of Departments)	
Corporation for National and Community Service	1.3
Corps of Engineers – Civil Works	4.6
Environmental Protection Agency	9
NASA	18.7

<u>National Intelligence Program</u>	<u>0.0?</u>
<u>Really?</u>	
National Science Foundation	7.8
Overseas Contingency Operations	126.7
Small Business Administration	.985
Social Security Administration	<u>12.5</u>
Total Projected Budget	1234.535

These figures are giving the Feds the benefit of the doubt. The Budget for the spies is??

The main conundrum here is why is the United States government requiring <u>all</u> states to comply with laws that may or may not be appropriate for any particular state? Why do they have the audacity to presume they know better how to manage people of a particular region, better than the governing body of the people specific to that locale, to say it in another way… "governments lead best when leading at the lowest possible level". If that statement is valid, then the state and local governments will be more responsive and understand better the situation within their states better than a bloated unresponsive government body made up of career politicians who really don't care about the plight of any specific area of the United States except for their constituency. For, as a career politician, the only future plans they have are for re-election and whatever their pet project is for their voter base (got to keep them happy). Why would a Representative from Indiana care about the influx of itinerant workers to Arizona? Wouldn't it be reasonable to suppose the people of Arizona have a better grasp on the situation in their state rather than relying on a state that doesn't have the same situations? This just screams for moving these challenges to the state and local level rather than looking to a federal government who has never had the information or the expertise to handle these unique problems.

Is there redundancy in our bureaucratic prone government system? Yes! Is it necessary? No. You only have to take a cursory glance at the budget categories to see that the majority of the departments are duplicates of the states' departments. So to what purpose do they serve? The only purpose I can imagine is to keep the states in line and generate copious amounts of revenue, it's all about control and money. All these agencies and Departments seem to do is threaten to withhold monies from the individual states who won't knuckle under to federal government mandates, whether they like it or not. i.e. Arizona...The feds sued the state of Arizona for passing a state law to do the job the feds were supposed to be doing, but were not.

Is this the way our government was originally organized? NO!!! Our federal government was originally developed to assist the states in affairs of a foreign nature as a singular image for the several states with other governments when these governments interacted with the federation of the states, only to give the federation one voice. This is inclusive with protection, international trade, immigration, and dealing as a mediator of interstate business. Not to dictate what our states should or should not do internally, that is a matter of local interest.

Let's look at the different departments and see if they are justified in their existence.

1. Agriculture – Now how many farmers are working in the federal government? Not many I would imagine and what position do they have in reference to growing, managing or marketing agriculture? All I really hear from the feds is how they are helping our farmers in times of strife. Or how they dole out subsidies so the farmer can survive. Well may be, but if the farmer needed subsidies to exist then they must be growing the wrong thing. That may sound harsh and unfeeling, but agriculture is a business just like any other business. Business succeeds and fails based upon the organization and management of the entity. Some make it, more don't. That's how business works and farming needs to run the same way. It will create a stronger and more profitable infrastructure. The main idea is we don't need the feds to tell our farmers how to run a farm or what to grow. Do away with this department and

there's 23.9 Billion dollars back to the American people in savings of their hard earned dollar.

2. Commerce – This does have an International contingent, so that section of the department may survive the cut, but not the domestic side. Again I ask what does the federal government know about Commerce, nothing...name one profitable enterprise the government ran that is still in existence. There are none. I say let the state and local governments manage commerce locally and the result will be that local commerce will be healthy and prosperous. The feds do nothing to encourage anything that would result in healthy business all they do is create laws to restrict business and innovation.

3. Defense – Here's one of the biggies...Most of us will agree, we do periodically need defense. It was one of the things that is specifically provided for in our Constitution. I concur, but...do we need so much? What I mean is, look at all of the foreign bases we currently occupy. Do we really need several thousand troops to be in Japan? What about Germany, England, Spain, Italy, Iceland, Greenland ...etc. This list is not all inclusive. We are complaining about getting out of Iraq and Afghanistan, but those troops are only a drop in the bucket. Worldwide we have literally Hundreds of Thousands maybe Millions of troops in foreign lands spending American cash that could be better used here in the good ole' USA. So let's bring them

home and if they aren't needed here then let's lessen the size of the combat force. Keep in mind these deployments were originally set up for a reason that may have made sense in the past, but times and circumstances have changed, so why don't we change with them?

4. Department of Energy – What does this department do? Since conjured up by President Jimmy Carter to "Try to get our country into a place to become free from foreign oil " It has no real job in the overall scheme of things, I mean how are they doing on that separation from dependence on foreign oil? Yeah, right!

5. How about the H's Departments Health and Human Services, Housing and Urban Development and last but certainly not least Homeland Security, basically 171.1 Billion for jobs that were already being accomplished either through other Departments or Agencies of the US Government or they are totally redundant.

Let me remind you that these ramblings of mine are only my personal observations and opinions. Each of these points will need to be put through the plan that is developed by the states and their implementation force. I could go through all the sections and comment on all these ridiculous situations but this is neither the time nor the place for redundancy. What the plan is for the various committees which are organized by the states is to look at these departments and agencies and make the determination whether they live, get modified or die.

We could go through all the Departments and agencies, but that is not what this dissertation is about. It's about the idea of getting these Departments and Agencies handled appropriately. That will be done by the Plan we already talked about. We can see, just by looking at the Budget how much of this budgeting is redundant and not useful. That is why I put this chapter in the book. I don't think Congress looks at whether there is any necessity for many of these areas of our government.

Why do we need a Department of Homeland Security...everything it is charged to do was already being done before it was organized.

What about Department of Education? Our educational system was actually more efficiently managed before it was instituted.

I could go on, but that is what the organization process will be about. So I will leave the rest to be hashed out through the Plan.

All I will say right now is let's get going, the sooner the better. We don't want to wait any longer. The longer we wait the more work it will be.

Now we get to everyone's favorite subject, how the feds finance their budget... taxes.

Taxes

My opinion on taxation in the United States: (mostly researched on Wikipedia)

Taxation history of the United States

Before 1776, the American Colonies were subject to taxation by the United Kingdom, and also imposed local taxes. Property taxes were imposed in the Colonies as early as 1634. In 1673, the UK Parliament imposed a tax on exports from the American Colonies, and with it created the first tax administration in what would become the United States. Other tariffs and taxes were imposed by Parliament. Most of the colonies and many localities adopted property taxes.

Under Article VIII of the Articles of Confederation, the United States Federal government did not have the power to tax. All such power lay with the states. The United States Constitution, adopted in 1787, authorized the Federal government to lay and collect taxes, but required that some types of tax revenues be given to the states in proportion to population. Tariffs were the principal Federal tax through the 1800s.

By 1796, state and local governments in fourteen of the 15 states taxed land. Delaware taxed the income from property. By the American Civil War, the principle of taxation of property at a uniform rate had developed, and many of the states relied on property taxes as a major source of revenue. However, the increasing importance of intangible property, such as corporate stock, caused the states to shift to other forms of taxation in the 1900s. Income taxes in the form of "faculty" taxes were imposed by the colonies. These combined income and property tax characteristics, and the income element persisted after 1776 in a few states. Several states adopted income taxes in 1837. Wisconsin adopted a corporate and individual income tax in 1911, and was the first to administer the tax with a state tax administration. The first Federal income tax was adopted as part of the Revenue Act of 1861. The tax lapsed after the American Civil War. Subsequently enacted income taxes were held to be unconstitutional by the Supreme Court because they were not given to the states. In 1913, the Sixteenth Amendment was ratified, permitting the Federal government to levy an income tax without giving all of it to the states.

The Federal income tax enacted in 1913 included corporate and individual income taxes. It defined income using language from prior laws, incorporated in the Sixteenth Amendment, as "all income from whatever source derived." The tax allowed deductions for business expenses, but few non-business deductions. In 1918 the income tax law was expanded to include a foreign tax credit and more comprehensive definitions of income and deduction items. Various aspects of the present system of definitions were expanded through 1926, when U.S. law was organized as the United States Code. Income, estate, gift, and excise tax provisions, plus provisions relating to tax returns and enforcement, were codified as Title 26, also known as the Internal Revenue Code. This was reorganized and somewhat expanded in 1954, and remains in the same general form.

Federal taxes were expanded greatly during World War I. In 1921, wealthy industrialist and then Treasury Secretary Andrew Mellon engineered a series of significant income tax cuts under three presidents. Mellon argued that tax cuts would spur growth. The last such cut in 1928 was followed by the Great Depression in 1929. Taxes were raised again in the latter part of the Depression, and during World War II. Income tax rates were reduced significantly during the Johnson, Nixon, and Reagan Presidencies. Significant tax cuts for corporations and upper income individuals were enacted during the second Bush Presidency.

In 1986, Congress adopted, with little modification, a major expansion of the income tax portion of the Internal Revenue Code proposed in 1985 by the U.S. Treasury Department under President Reagan. The thousand page Tax Reform Act of 1986 significantly lowered tax rates, adopted sweeping expansions of international rules, eliminated the lower individual tax rate for capital gains, added significant inventory accounting rules, and made substantial other expansions of the law.

Federal income tax rates have been modified frequently. Tax rates were changed in 34 of the 97 years between 1913 and 2010. The rate structure has been graduated since the 1913 act.

The first individual income tax return Form 1040 under the 1913 law was four pages long. In 1915, some Congressmen complained about the complexity of the form. In 1921,

Congress considered but did not enact replacement of the income tax with a national sales tax.

By the 1920s, many states had adopted income taxes on individuals and corporations. Many of the state taxes were simply based on the Federal definitions. The states generally taxed residents on all of their income, including income earned in other states, as well as income of nonresidents earned in the state. This led to a long line of Supreme Court cases limiting the ability of states to tax income of nonresidents.

The states had also come to rely heavily on retail sales taxes. However, as of the beginning of World War II, only two cities (New York and New Orleans) had local sales taxes.

The Federal Estate Tax was introduced in 1916, and Gift Tax in 1924. Unlike many inheritance taxes, the Gift and Estate taxes were imposed on the transferor rather than the recipient. Many states adopted either inheritance taxes or estate and gift taxes, often computed as the amount allowed as a deduction for Federal purposes. These taxes remained under 1% of government revenues through the 1990s.

The Federal and all the States Governments within the United States provide tax exemption for some income, property, or persons. These exemptions have their roots both in tax theory, Federal and state legislative history, and the Constitution of the United States.

The United States is a federal republic with autonomous state and local governments. Taxes are imposed in the United States at each of these levels. These include taxes on income, property, sales, imports, payroll, estates and gifts, as well as various fees.

Taxes are imposed on net income of individuals and corporations by the federal, most state, and some local governments. Residents are taxed on worldwide income and allowed a credit for foreign taxes. Income subject to tax is determined under tax rules, not accounting principles, and includes almost all income from whatever source. Most business expenses reduce taxable income, though limits apply to a few expenses. Individuals are permitted to reduce taxable income by personal allowances and certain nonbusiness expenses, including home mortgage interest, state and local taxes, charitable contributions, and medical and certain other expenses incurred above certain percentages of income. State rules for determining taxable income often differ from federal rules. Federal tax rates vary from 15% to 35% of taxable income. State and local tax rates vary by jurisdiction, and many are graduated. State taxes are generally treated as a deductible expense for federal tax computation. Certain alternative taxes may apply.

It is understood that taxes are necessary to run the various machinations of the Federal, State and local government operations. We as a society have several services we require in order to function as a people. We must have laws therefore we need a system to make and insure the carrying out of and adherence to those laws. We all need certain levels of assistance such as fire protection, security, and health assistance. These are services we can all agree are needed in today's society and for which most of us are willing to pay our governments. There are however, several other functions of government for which our federal government is providing because IT says we need a selected function because they say so and we have no say so as to whether we want that particular system or agency. So why do I oppose taxes? I don't. I oppose the idea that our government can impose these taxes on us without our say so and that they can get the taxes from wherever they deem necessary. So the answer is…do we need it? Yes. Can we develop a method to control how it's being used? Yes!

Having said that, I will give a run down on where the government gets their money. To some of us this maybe illuminating, I know it was for me. The scary thing is that much of this money is essentially not accounted for. We don't know how much the government collects and what they do for this money. So, here are the taxes I have researched. Is there more…probably. I just haven't found them.

Payroll taxes

Payroll taxes are imposed by the federal and all state governments. These include Social Security and Medicare taxes imposed on both employers and employees, at a combined rate of 15.3% (13.3% for 2011). Social Security tax applies only to the first $106,800 of wages in 2009 through 2011. Employers also must withhold income taxes on wages. An unemployment tax and certain other levies apply and FICA.

Property taxes

Property taxes are imposed by most local governments and many special purpose authorities based on the fair market value of property. School and other authorities are often separately governed, and impose separate taxes. Property tax is generally imposed only on realty, though some jurisdictions tax some forms of business property. Property tax rules and rates vary widely.

Sales taxes are imposed on the price at retail sale of many goods and some services by most states and some localities. Sales tax rates vary widely among jurisdictions, from 0% to 16%, and may vary within a jurisdiction based on the particular goods or services taxed. Sales tax is collected by the seller at the time of sale, or remitted as use tax by buyers of taxable items who did not pay sales tax.

The United States imposes tariffs or customs duties on the import of many types of goods from many jurisdictions. This tax must be paid before the goods can be legally imported. Rates of duty vary from 0% to more than 20%, based on the particular goods and country of origin.

Investment Taxes

Capital gains tax
In the United States, with certain exceptions, individuals and corporations pay income tax on the net total of all their capital gains. Short-term capital gains are taxed at a higher rate: the ordinary income tax rate. The tax rate for individuals on "long-term capital gains", which are gains on assets that have been held for over one year before being sold, is lower than the ordinary income tax rate, and in some tax brackets there is no tax due on such gains. The tax rate on long-term gains was reduced in 2003 to 15% (for individuals, whose highest tax bracket is 15% or more), or to 5% for individuals in the lowest two income tax brackets (whose highest tax bracket is less than 15%). The reduced 15% tax rate on eligible dividends and capital gains, previously scheduled to expire in 2008, has been extended through 2010 as a result of the Tax Increase Prevention and Reconciliation Act signed into law by President Bush on May 17, 2006, which also reduced the 5% rate to 0%. Toward the end of 2010, President Obama signed a law

extending the reduced rate on eligible dividends until the end of 2012.

Import tax (Tariffs)

Tariffs for many years were primarily to collect federal revenue and only secondarily to protect start-up industries. Since the government largely restricted its activities to maintaining order and protecting property via the army, navy and courts tariffs raised enough revenues to finance the government. During wars or to meet other needs additional income was secured by raising the tariff and excise tax rates. Short term and unanticipated capital needs (budget deficits) are usually covered by borrowing.

A protective Tariff is often used by governments to attempt to control trade between nations to protect and encourage their noncompetitive or undeveloped local industries, businesses, unions etc. giving them time to become competitive. The reasons for an industry or business being noncompetitive are basically four:

- Their average wages may be higher than is typical in the competitor's country.
- They do not have the innovations or inventions that their competitors have.
- They do not have the skill sets or organization their competitors have.
- They lack raw materials needed to make some product.

Tariff rates are set up many times to "punish" trade tariffs, etc., on U.S. goods passed by other countries who are trying to protect their uncompetitive industries and/or businesses. It is unclear whether this policy works very well because the lack of competition often encourages companies (and governments) to keep inefficient and out dated equipment or business practices. These protected industries are often uncompetitive on the non-domestic market. Without the tariffs the customers can buy imported products cheaper and force the local companies to become more competitive. Tariffs are nearly always imposed on imported foreign goods and very seldom on exported goods and nearly always cost the consumer extra money. Historically U.S. tariffs on imported goods and products till 1913 ranged from 8% to 45% (averaging about 22%) and the collected tariff income supported nearly all the Federal Governments expenses until the Sixteenth Amendment allowing Federal Income Taxes was passed in 1913.

In the 18th and 19th centuries, many countries primary source of income was import tariffs. Tariffs tended to be lowered as other sources of tax income like income taxes, payroll taxes, value-added taxes (VAT), property taxes, sales tax, etc. have been enacted. In the United States property taxes and sales tax have nearly always been reserved for state and local government income sources. Various Income Tax rates and schedules are also common in many states but tariffs are not. Tariffs in the U.S. can only be imposed only by the Federal government at a uniform rate and not by state or local governments.

Presently only about 30% of all import goods are subject to tariffs in the United States, the rest are on the free list. The "average" tariffs now charged by the United States are at a historic low. The list of negotiated tariffs are listed on the Harmonized Tariff Schedule as put out by the United States International Trade Commission.

The U.S. Customs and Border Protection (CBP) is a federal law enforcement agency of the United States Department of Homeland Security charged with regulating and facilitating international trade, collecting customs (import duties or tariffs approved by the U.S. Congress), and enforcing U.S. regulations, including trade, customs and immigration. They man most border crossing stations and ports. When shipments of goods arrive at a border crossing or port, customs officers inspect the contents and charge a tax according to the tariff formula for that product. Usually the goods cannot continue on their way until the custom duty is paid. Custom duties are one the easiest taxes to collect, and the cost of collection is small. Traders seeking to evade tariffs are known as smugglers and can be fines or sent tp prison.

	Tariff Income	Receipts % Tariff	Federal Receipts	Income Tax	Payroll Tax	Receipts % Excise
2010	$25,298.0	1.2%	$2,162,700.0	$1,090,000.0	$864,800.0	3.1%

Note: each dollar income is stated in millions of dollars

Estate tax

The Federal *estate tax* is imposed "on the transfer of the taxable estate of every decedent who is a citizen or resident of the United States." The starting point in the calculation is the "gross estate." Certain deductions (subtractions) from the "gross estate" amount are allowed in arriving at a smaller amount called the "taxable estate." The question here is how much money does the US make each year in Estate tax?

(note: I couldn't find any figures on the amount of taxes collected per year).

The "gross estate"

The "gross estate" for Federal estate tax purposes often includes more property than that included in the "probate estate" under the property laws of the state in which the decedent lived at the time of death. The gross estate (before the modifications) may be considered to be the value of all the property interests of the decedent at the time of death. To these interests are added the following property interests generally not owned by the decedent at the time of death:

- the value of property to the extent of an interest held by the surviving spouse as a "dower or curtsey"
- the value of certain items of property in which the decedent had, at any time, made a transfer during the three years immediately preceding the date of death (i.e., even if the property was no longer owned by the decedent on the date of death), other than certain gifts, and other than property sold for full value;

- the value of certain property transferred by the decedent before death for which the decedent retained a "life estate", or retained certain "powers";
- the value of certain property in which the recipient could, through ownership, have possession or enjoyment only by surviving the decedent;
- the value of certain property in which the decedent retained a "reversionary interest", the value of which exceeded five percent of the value of the property;
- the value of certain property transferred by the decedent before death where the transfer was revocable;
- the value of certain annuities;
- the value of certain jointly owned property, such as assets passing by operation of law or survivorship, i.e. joint tenants with rights of survivorship or tenants by the entirety, with special rules for assets owned jointly by spouses.;
- the value of certain "powers of appointment";
- the amount of proceeds of certain life insurance policies.

Gift tax

A gift tax is a tax imposed on the gratuitous transfer of ownership of property. The United States Internal Revenue Service says a gift is "Any transfer to an individual, either directly or indirectly, where full consideration (measured in money or money's worth) is not received in return."
(Note collection figures here either.)

Luxury tax

When a luxury tax is imposed, the majority of people aren't affected by it and aren't subject to the tax.[1] Over time, what is viewed as "luxury" might change, resulting in more and more people being affected by the tax. Despite the animosity that ensues, the government may view the income from the luxury tax as essential and will not restrict or rescind it. So it may happen over time that goods considered "ordinary" might also incur luxury tax. An example of this can be seen with various commodities in the country of Norway, where at the beginning of last century, cars and chocolate were viewed as luxury goods. Thus, additional taxes were levied upon these goods. Today few Norwegians consider cars or chocolate a luxury, but the luxury taxes on these goods remain. In Ireland, many personal hygiene products are within the luxury tax bracket. In the United States, winning on a game show is usually considered a luxury, which is subject to taxation as well. This tax rate will be more than standard income tax. (again no annual figures)

Telecommunications tax

Federal Subscriber Line Charge:
Also known as: Federal Access Charge, Customer Line Charge, Interstate Access Charge, Interstate Single Line Charge, FCC Approved Customer Line Charge, Subscriber Line Charge or SLC) Federal Subscriber Line Charge: The Local exchange carriers (LECs) are authorized to bill a Federal Subscriber Line Charge fee. These fees can be as low as $3 or as high as $7 per line depending on the local

carrier. They are designed to recover cost for access to the long distance network. Some long distance carriers charge their customers various fees on a per line basis but these fees are not mandated, they're another way for the carrier to add revenue. Remember, when contracting for local and long distance telecommunications service, everything is negotiable. This federally ordered charge billed by your local telephone company pays part of the cost to the local telephone company of supplying a phone line into your home or business. This recouped money is designed to help local phone companies recover the cost of providing "local loops" which refers to outside telephone wires, underground conduit, telephone poles, and other equipment and facilities connecting you to the telephone network. It is a charge that is part of the price you pay to your local telephone company but it is not an actual mandated tax and revenues for it are not sent in to any government entity. The FCC places a maximum cap on this charge. See the FCC website for more information.

Federal Excise tax or Federal User tax

This tax appears on your local phone bills. It is charged as a set percentage regardless of which telephone service provider you use. The majority of this tax was nearly completely eliminated in 2007 and many companies were refunded previous payments on long distance and cell phone excise taxes by the Internal Revenue Service. The tax still appears minimally on local telephone usage charges and cell phone charges.

Federal Subscriber Line Charge or Federal Access Charge, Customer Line Charge, Interstate Access Charge, Interstate Single Line Charge, FCC Approved Customer Line Charge, Subscriber Line Charge or SLC)

This federally ordered charge billed by your local telephone company pays part of the cost to the local telephone company of supplying a phone line into your home or business. It is designed to help local phone companies recover the cost of providing "local loops" which refers to outside telephone wires, underground conduit, telephone poles, and other equipment and facilities connecting you to the telephone network. This is NOT a tax. It is a charge that is part of the price you pay to your local telephone company. Neither the FCC nor any other government agency receives the Federal Subscriber Line Charge. The FCC places a maximum cap on this charge. Currently, as of July 1st, 2002, the FCC places a maximum on this charge of $6.00 for the first line and the lower of actual costs or $7.00 for non-primary lines in residences. For multi-line businesses the maximum allowed is the lower of actual costs or $9.20 per line.

Long distance PICC Fees:

Also known on your phone bill as: National Access Fee, LD Line Charge, Presubscribed Interexchange Carrier Charge, Carrier Line Charge. Presubscribed Line Charge, Regulatory Related Charge, FCC Primary Carrier 1st Line. This long distance portion charge started on January 1, 1998 as part of the FCC overhaul of telephone fees. Long distance companies pay a flat fee to the local telephone company when you pre-subscribe your telephone line to their long distance service. The charge is designed to compensate the local telephone companies for the costs associated with providing "local loop" service. If a consumer or business has not selected a long distance company for its telephone lines, the local telephone company may bill for the PICC. Although every long distance company is charged the same flat rate per line, long distance companies are allowed to pass on this charge using disguised methodology, and each company uses a different method to charge this *carrier specific* fee. Although it does not appear negotiable, it often is. Some telecom providers do not charge this fee at all, and some charge a "carrier specific" flat fee. This is NOT a tax. Please note that on July 1, 2000 the FCC ruled that long distance companies no longer will have to pay this fee to local companies for residential lines, or single line businesses, therefore no longer something the carriers should ethically pass on. The charge continues for multiple line businesses. Many long distance companies are still charging customers for this, although though they aren't paying it anymore as a pass on to the local telephone companies.

Taking all these various charges into account, how much does the feds report on their budgetary income? I can't find out.

Excise taxes

Excise duties or taxes often serve political as well as financial ends. Public safety and health, public morals, environmental protection, and national defense are all legitimate rationales for the imposition of an excise.

- **Public safety and health** –
  - deter individuals from harming their health by abusing substances such as tobaco and alcohol, thus making excise a kind of sumptuary tax, or
  - deter them from engaging in morally objectionable activities such as gambling and prostitution ,thus making it a type of vice tax or sin tax
- **Environmental protection** -
  - deter individuals or organizations from harming the general environment, including curbing activities which contribute to pollution, or which harm the natural environment.

- **Defense - including taxation directly levied on other countries' militaries and/or governments, such as the UK's taxation on "visiting forces"**

- **Punitive** - Many US states tax on drugs. These taxes are not considered revenue sources, but rather exist to allow governments greater leverage for punishments and reparations/war reparations - based mainly around tax evasion - which can be imposed in the event that the perpetrator is caught and tried.

    Federal Excise taxes have a storied background in the United States. Responding to an urgent need for revenue following the American Revolutionary War, after passage of the U.S. Constitution the First United States Congress passed, and President George Washington, signed the Tariff Act of July 4, 1789, which authorized the collection of duties on imported goods. Customs duties as set by tariff rates up to 1860 were usually about 80-95% of all federal revenue. Having just fought a war over taxation (among other things) the U.S. Congress wanted a reliable source of income that was relatively unobtrusive and easy to collect. Tariffs and excise taxes were authorized by the United States Constitution and recommended by the first U.S. Treasury Secretary, Alexander Hamilton in 1789 to tax foreign imports and set up low excise taxes to provide the Federal Government with enough money to pay its operating expenses and to redeem at full value U.S. Federal debts and the debts the states had accumulated during the American Revolutionary War. Hamilton thought it was important to start the U.S. Federal government out on a sound financial basis with good credit. The first Federal budget was about $4.6 million dollars and the population in the 1790 U.S. Census was about four million. Hence the average federal tax was about $1/person per year. Then tradesmen earned about $0.25 a day for a 10-12 hour day so federal taxes could be paid with about four days work. Paying even this was usually optional as taxed imports listed on the tariff lists could usually be avoided if desired.

The Congress set low excise taxes on only a few goods, such as, whiskey, rum, tobacco, snuff and refined sugar. There were initially no other significant sources of federal income besides tariffs. The excise tax on whiskey was so despised it led to the Whiskey Rebellion which had to be quelled by Washington calling up the Militia and repressing the rebellious farmers--all were later pardoned. The whiskey excise tax collected so little and was so despised it was abolished by President Thomas Jefferson in 1802. In the Napoleonic Wars and the War of 1812 the imports to the United States plummeted and the Congress in 1812 brought back the excise tax on whiskey to compensate for the loss of customs revenue. Within a few years customs duties (tariff) brought in enough federal income to again abolish nearly all federal excise taxes. When the United States public debt was finally paid off in 1834 President Andrew Jackson kept the excise tax zeroed out and reduced the customs duties (tariffs) in half.

Excise taxes stayed essentially zero till the U.S. Civil War brought a need for much more federal revenue. Excise taxes were reintroduced on a wider range of items and Income taxes (later declared unconstitutional) were introduced. By about 1916 the loans taken out during the Civil War were all paid off and the excise taxes were again set very low. On January 16, 1919 the 18th Amendment was passed and alcohol production, sale and transport were essentially prohibited. Taxing alcohol products would have produced almost no income. Excise taxes remained essentially zero for the next ten years.

During the Great Depression (1929-1939) President Franklin Roosevelt and Congress started reintroducing excise taxes to increase federal income which had dropped because of the much lower income tax collections. On December 5, 1933 the 21st Amendment was ratified and alcohol production became legal again. The healthy excise tax on now legal alcoholic beverages paid about one-third of all federal taxes during the Great Depression.

Excise taxes now have become an established part of the general budget as well as the source of funds for various trusts. The U.S. has expanded the definition of items on the excise tax lists as trusts for highways, airports, vaccines, black lung, oil spills, etc. have been set up. These are financed by excise taxes on fuels, tickets, vaccines, coal, oil etc.

Excise taxes are generally taxes on events like the purchase of a quantity of a particular item like: gasoline, diesel fuel, liquor, wine, cigarettes, airline tickets, tires, trucks, etc. and are usually included in the price of the item—not listed separately like sales taxes usually are. To minimize tax accounting complications, the excise tax is usually imposed on quantities like gallons of fuel, gallons of wine or drinking alcohol, packets of cigarettes, etc. and are usually paid initially by the manufacturer or retailer. All excise taxes are, of course, passed on to the consumer who eventually *consumes* the product. The price the item is eventually sold for is not generally considered in calculating the excise taxes. Income taxes, value added taxes (VATS), sales taxes, and transfer taxes are all examples of other event taxes but are typically not called excise taxes (in the U.S.) because of the different ways they are assessed. In the U.S. essentially the only taxes called excise taxes are the taxes on quantities of enumerated items (whiskey, wine, tobacco, gasoline, tires, etc.). Other *events* may *technically* be considered *excise taxes* but are seldom collected under that name. An example of a *state of being* tax is an ad valorem property tax—which is not an excise. Customs or tariffs are based on the property (usually imported goods) as a *state of being* or Ad-valorem taxes and are also typically not called excise taxes. Excise taxes are collected by producers and retailers and paid to the Internal Revenue Service or other state and/or local government tax collection agency.

Historical federal excise tax collections to 1945 are listed in the *Historical Statistics of the United States* and more recent federal excise tax data is listed in the White House historical tables.

U.S. 2010 Excise Tax Rates

Item	Tax Rate	Measure
General Fund Excise taxes		
Small Cigarettes	$1.01	pkg 20
Cigars, large	$0.40	ea. cigar
Distilled Alcohol 80 proof	$2.14	750 ml
Wine 14% Alcohol or Less	$0.21	750 ml
Wine 14 to 21%	$0.31	750 ml
Wine 21 to 24%	$0.62	750 ml
Wine Sparkling	$0.67	750 ml
Wine Carbonated	$0.65	750 ml
Hard Cider	$0.04	750 ml
Beer	$0.05	12 oz
Pistols and Revolvers	10%	price
er Firearms and Ammunitior	11%	price
Tanning Salon	10%	price
Gas guzzler 21.5-22.5 mpg	1,000.00	vehicle
Gas guzzler 12.5-13.5 mpg	6,400.00	vehicle
Telephone Calls	3%	local
Wagering excise tax	2.50%	wager
Black Lung Disability Trust		
Coal mined	$1.10	ton
Coal mined	4.40%	price
Coal open pit	$0.55	ton
Coal open pit	4.40%	price
Highway Trust Fund		
Gasoline	$0.183	gallon
Diesel	$0.243	gallon
Alcohol fuels	$0.183	gallon
LPG fuel	$0.183	gallon
LNG fuel	$0.243	gallon

CNG fuel	$0.183	gallon
Tires over 3,500 lb. rated wt.	$0.09	10# rated wt
Heavy Trucks	12%	price
55,000–75,000 lbs. capacity	$100.00	truck/yr.
each 1000# over 55,000	$22.00	truck/yr.
over 75,000 #	$550.00	truck/yr.

Leaking Underground Storage Tank Trust

Leaking Gas storage	.1 cent	gallon

Vaccine Injury Compensation Trust Fund Excise

Vaccine	$0.75	dose

Water Transportation Passenger excise tax

Ship voyage	$3.00	passenger

Land and Water Conservation Trust Fund

Ship fuel	$0.20	gallon

Oil Spill fund

Oil	$0.08	barrel

Harbor Maintenance Trust Fund

Harbor Maintenance	0.13%	cargo

Sport Fish Restoration & Boating Trust Fund

Sport Fishing gear	10%	price
Boat Gasoline	$0.183	gallon
Boat Diesel	$0.243	gallon

Airport and Airway Trust Fund

Airline Ticket	7.50%	price
International Ticket	$16.30	ea.
Air Cargo	6.25%	charges
Comm. Aviation kerosene	$0.043	gallon
Jet Fuel	$0.218	gallon
Aviation gasoline	$0.194	gallon

Notes:

Some Excise taxes are assigned to Trust Funds and are collected for and "dedicated" to the Trust.

For purposes of the U.S. Constitution, an excise tax can be defined as any indirect tax, or event tax. An excise means any tax *other than*: (1) a property tax or Ad-valorem tax by reason of its ownership; (2) a tax per head tax or capitation tax by being present (very rare in the U.S.); (3) an income tax paid directly to the government on income; or a (4) sales tax which is paid on all sales except specifically exempted items. An excise is imposed on listed specific taxable events or products and are usually not collected or paid directly by the consumer--a direct tax. Excise taxes are collected by the producer or retailer and paid by them to the Internal Revenue Service, state or local tax agency. Of course the consumer ultimately pays the excise tax which is added to the price of the product when it is sold. Often sales taxes are collected as a percentage of the cost of the product and its excise tax--a tax on a tax!

The excise taxes on alcoholic beverages, tobacco products and firearms are administered under the Alcohol and Tobacco Tax and Trade Bureau (TTB) in the United States Department of the Treasury. The total excise taxes on gasoline, diesel etc. for each state have been calculated. The differing excise taxes in each state on fuels are given in the wikipedia article Fuel taxes in the United States. The differing excise taxes in each state on cigarettes are given in the wikipedia article Cigarette taxes in the United States.

Federal Trust Fund excise tax collections are often remitted to each state by complicated allocation plans. The Highway Trust fund moneys are split between highways and transit systems. The Highway Account normally receives about

85% of all highway trust fund taxes, and the Mass Transit Account receives about 15% of all Highway Trust Fund excise tax collections. The Highway Trust Fund may well require tax rate adjustments to stay solvent and make up for the increased car mileage dictated by the EPA or the increased use of untaxed electric vehicles. As fuel prices increase, there is a slow decrease in gallons of fuel bought as vehicles are made more efficient and/or travel smaller distances all of which reduce Highway Trust Fund collections. Federal funding of the Highway Trust Fund is restricted for use on capital expenditures, such as construction and reconstruction of roads, bridges or tunnels, or payment of bonds sold to finance the work. The bulk of funding is for specific programs set up to channel aid to the States for a variety of uses, such as providing capital funding for the Nation's most heavily used roads, maintaining interstates, and fixing bridges. Regular maintenance on non-interstate roads, including pothole patching and snowplowing, must be funded through other sources. Funding often requires a partial dollar match by the states. The Mass Transit Account which gets its funding from a fraction of the excise taxes imposed on fuels, etc. has similar restrictions.

Statutory law

The term "excise" also has a **statutory law** meaning. Generally, in the United States any statute that imposes a tax specifically denominated as an "excise" is an excise tax law. U.S. Federal statutory excises are (or have been) imposed under Subtitle D ("miscellaneous excise taxes") and Subtitle E ("Alcohol, Tobacco, and Certain Other Excise Taxes") of the Internal Revenue Code, 26 U.S.C. § 4001 through 26 U.S.C. § 5891, relating to such things as luxury passenger automobiles, heavy trucks and trailers, "gas guzzler" vehicles, tires, petroleum products, coal, vaccines, recreational equipment, firearms, communications services air transportation, policies issued by foreign insurance companies, wagering, water transportation, removal of hard mineral resources from deep sea beds, chemicals, certain imported substances, non-deductible contributions to certain employer plans, and many other subjects.

Excise duties usually have one or two purposes: to raise revenue and to discourage particular behavior or purchase of particular items. Taxes such as those on sales of fuel, alcohol and tobacco are often "justified" on both grounds. Some economists suggest that the optimal revenue raising taxes should be levied on sales of items having an inelastic demand, while behavior altering taxes should be levied where demand is elastic. Most items on the excise tax lists are relatively inelastic "addictions" with only long term elasticity.

One of the most common excises in the United States is the cigarette tax imposed by both the states and federal governments. This tax is simply an excise tax applied to each pack of cigarettes. Specifically, the federal government uniformly charges an excise tax of $1.01 for a standard pack of 20 cigarettes. On top of the federal tax, all 50 states levy a different cigarette tax that ranges from $0.17 per pack in Missouri to $4.35 per pack in New York. Overall, the excise taxes constitute most of the retail cost of cigarettes. Cigarette taxes can be avoided in some jurisdictions if the consumer purchases loose tobacco and cigarette paper separately or by purchase of cigarettes from lower taxed states.

Excise taxes can be imposed and collected at the point of production or importation, or at the point of sale and then remitted to the Internal Revenue Service or state or local taxing agency. Often some excise taxes are collected by the federal government and then remitted to the states on a partially matching basis to pay for particular items like interstate highway construction, airport construction or bridge repairs. Excise taxes are usually waived or refunded on goods being exported, so as to encourage exports. Smugglers and other tax avoiders will often seek to obtain items at a point at which they are not taxed or taxed much lower and then later sell or use them at a price lower than the post-tax price in their jurisdiction.

For similar items, excise duties are the same for imported and domestically produced goods; if the tax is different, then there is an explicit or implicit customs duty or tariff.

Tourism tax

Transient occupancy tax (TOT), hotel/motel occupancy tax (HOT), tourist tax, tourist development tax, permissive lodging tax, lodging facility use tax, bed tax, room occupancy tax, gross receipts meal tax, mixed drink tax, restaurant tax, "bed, board, beverage" aka BBB tax, license recoupment fee, state rental surcharge, concession recovery fee and airport facility/access fees are various monikers used to collect additional funds from travelers. These taxes and fees are "generally" designated to fund tourism marketing organizations (CVBs/DMOs), but as you will so often find that is not always the case.
(Can't find any figures here,)

The following categories are areas where the government gets tax fees but again I can't find any info on how much they take in yearly or seem to be earmarked for specific uses.

Personal Holding Company tax
Passive Foreign Company tax
Controlled Foreign Corporation tax

Estate and gift tax

Estate and gift taxes in the United States are imposed by the Federal and most state governments. The estate tax is an excise tax levied on the right to pass property at death. It is imposed on the estate, not the beneficiary. Some states impose an inheritance tax on recipients of bequests. Gift taxes are levied on the giver (donor) of property where the property is transferred for less than adequate consideration. An additional generation-skipping transfer (GST) tax is imposed by the Federal and some state governments on transfers to grandchildren (or their descendants).

The Federal gift tax is computed based on cumulative taxable gifts, and is reduced by prior gift taxes paid. The Federal estate tax is computed on the sum of taxable estate and taxable gifts, and is reduced by prior gift taxes paid. These taxes are computed as the taxable amount times a graduated tax rate (up to 35% in 2011). The estate and gift taxes are also reduced by a "unified credit" equivalent to an exclusion ($5 million in 2011). Rates and exclusions have varied, and the benefits of lower rates and the credit have been phased out during some years.

Taxable gifts are certain gifts of U.S. property by nonresidents, most gifts of any property by residents, in excess of an annual exclusion ($13,000 for gifts made in 2011) per donor per donee. Taxable estates are certain U.S. property of nonresident decedents, and most property of residents. Residence for estate tax purposes is primarily based on domicile. U.S. real estate and most tangible property in the U.S. are subject to estate and gift tax whether the decedent or donor is resident or nonresident.

The taxable amount of a gift is the fair market value of the property in excess of consideration received at the date of gift. The taxable amount of an estate is the gross fair market value of all rights considered property at the date of death (or an alternative valuation date) ("gross estate"), less liabilities of the decedent, costs of administration (including funeral expenses) and certain other deductions. State estate taxes are deductible, with limitations, in computing the Federal taxable estate. Bequests to charities reduce the taxable estate.

Gift tax applies to all irrevocable transfers of interests in tangible or intangible property. Estate tax applies to all property owned in whole or in part by a citizen or resident at the time of his or her death, to the extent of the interest in the property. Generally, all types of property are subject to estate tax. Whether a decedent has sufficient interest in property for the property to be subject to gift or estate tax is determined under applicable state property laws. Certain interests in property that lapse at death (such as life insurance) are included in the taxable estate.

Taxable values of estates and gifts are the fair market value. For some assets, such as widely traded stocks and bonds, the value may be determined by market listings. The value of other property may be determined by appraisals, which are subject to potential contest by the taxing authority. Special use valuation applies to farms and closely held businesses, subject to limited dollar amount and other conditions. Monetary assets, such as cash, mortgages, and notes, are valued at the face amount, unless another value is clearly established.

Life insurance proceeds are included in the gross estate. The value of a right of a beneficiary of an estate to receive an annuity is included in the gross estate. Certain transfers during lifetime may be included in the gross estate. Certain powers of a decedent to control the disposition of property by another are included in the gross estate.

The taxable estate of a married decedent is reduced by a deduction for all property passing to the decedent's spouse. Certain terminable interests are included. Other conditions may apply.

Donors of gifts in excess of the annual exclusion must file gift tax returns on IRS form 709 and pay the tax. Executors of estates with a gross value in excess of the unified credit must file an estate tax return on IRS form 706 and pay the tax from the estate. Returns are required if the gifts or gross estate exceed the exclusions. Each state has its own forms and filing requirements. Tax authorities may examine and adjust gift and estate tax returns.

Licenses and occupational taxes

Many jurisdictions within the United States impose taxes or fees on the privilege of carrying on a particular business or maintaining a particular professional certification. These licensing or occupational taxes may be a fixed dollar amount per year for the licensee, an amount based on the number of practitioners in the firm, a percentage of revenue, or any of several other bases. Persons providing professional or personal services are often subject to such fees. Common examples include accountants, attorneys, barbers, casinos, dentists, doctors, auto mechanics, plumbers, and stock brokers. In addition to the tax, other requirements may be imposed for licensure.

All 50 states impose vehicle license fee. Generally, the fees are based on type and size of vehicle and are imposed annually or biannually. All states and the District of Columbia also impose a fee for a driver's license, which generally must be renewed with payment of fee every few years.

User fees

Fees are often imposed by governments for use of certain facilities or services. Such fees are generally imposed at the time of use. Multi-use permits may be available. For example, fees are imposed for use of national or state parks, rulings from the Internal Revenue Service, use of certain highways (called "tolls" or toll roads), parking on public streets, and use of public transit.

Tax administration

Taxes in the United States are administered by literally hundreds of tax authorities. At the Federal level there are three tax administrations. Alcohol, tobacco, and firearms taxes are administered by the Alcohol and Tobacco Tax and Trade Bureau (TTB). All other taxes on domestic activities are administered by the Internal Revenue Services (IRS). Taxes on imports (customs duties) are administered by U.S. Customs and Border Patrol. TTB is part of the Department of Justice and CBP belongs to the Department of Homeland Security. The IRS is a division within the U.S. Department of Treasury. Organization of state and local tax administrations varies widely. Every state maintains a tax administration. A few states administer some local taxes in whole or part. Most localities also maintain a tax administration or share one with neighboring localities.

Federal Internal Revenue Service

The IRS administers all U.S. Federal taxation on domestic activities, except those taxes administered by TTB. IRS functions include:

- Processing Federal tax returns (except TTB returns), including those for Social Security and other Federal payroll taxes
- Providing assistance to taxpayers in completing tax returns
- Collecting all taxes due related to such returns
- Enforcement of tax laws through examination of returns and assessment of penalties
- Providing an appeals mechanism for Federal tax disputes
- Referring matters to the Justice Department for prosecution
- Publishing information about U.S. Federal taxes, including forms, publications, and other materials
- Providing written guidance in the form of rulings binding on the IRS for the public and for particular taxpayers

The IRS maintains several Service Centers at which tax returns are processed. Taxpayers generally file most types of tax returns by mail with these Service Centers or file electronically. The IRS also maintains a National Office in Washington, DC, and numerous local offices providing taxpayer services and administering tax examinations.

Alcohol and Tobacco Tax and Trade Bureau

The Alcohol and Tobacco Tax Trade Bureau (TTB), a division of the Department of the Treasury, enforces Federal excise tax laws related to alcohol, tobacco, and firearms. TTB is organized as six divisions, each with discrete functions:

- Revenue Center: processes tax returns and issues permits, and related activities;
- Risk Management: internally develops guidelines and monitors programs;
- Tax Audit: verifies filing and payment of taxes;
- Trade Investigations: investigating arm for non-tobacco items; and
- Tobacco Enforcement Division: enforcement actions for tobacco; and
- Advertising, Labeling and Formulation Division: implements various labeling and ingredient monitoring.

Customs and Border Protection

U.S. Customs and Border Protection (CBP), an agency of the United States Department of Homeland Security, collects customs duties and regulates international trade. It has a workforce of over 58,000 employees covering over 300 official ports of entry to the United States. CBP has authority to seize and dispose of cargo in the case of certain violations of customs rules.

State administrations

Every state in the United States has its own tax administration subject to the rules of that state's law and regulations. These are referred to in most states as the Department of Revenue or Department of Taxation. The powers of the state taxing authorities vary widely. Most enforce all state level taxes but not most local taxes. However, many states have unified state-level sales tax administration, including for local sales taxes.

State tax returns are filed separately with those tax administrations, not with the Federal tax administrations. Each state has its own procedural rules, which vary widely.

Local administrations

Most localities within the United States administer most of their own taxes. In many cases, there are multiple local taxing jurisdictions with respect to a particular taxpayer or property. For property taxes, the taxing jurisdiction is typically represented by a tax assessor/collector whose offices are located at the taxing jurisdiction's facilities.

Legal basis

The United States Constitution provides that Congress "shall have the power to lay and collect Taxes, Duties, Imposts, and Excises ... but all Duties, Imposts, and Excises shall be uniform throughout the United States." Prior to amendment, it provided that "No Capitation, or other direct, Tax shall be Laid unless in proportion to the Census ..." The 16th Amendment provided that "Congress shall have the power to lay and collect taxes on incomes, from whatever source derived, without apportionment among the several States, and without regard to any census or enumeration." The 10th Amendment provided that "powers not delegated to the United States by this Constitution, nor prohibited to the States, are reserved to the States respectively, or to the people."

Congress has enacted numerous laws dealing with taxes since adoption of the Constitution. Those laws are now codified as Titlem19, Customs Duties, Title 26, Internal Revenue Code, and various other provisions. These laws specifically authorize the United States Secretary of the Treasury to delegate various powers related to levy, assessment and collection of taxes.

State constitutions uniformly grant the state government the right to levy and collect taxes. Limitations under state constitutions vary widely.

Various individuals and groups have questioned the legitimacy of United States federal income tax. These arguments are varied, but have been uniformly rejected by the Internal Revenue Service and by the courts and ruled to be frivolous.

Progressivity in United States income tax

Each major type of tax in the United States has been used by some jurisdiction at some time as a tool of social policy. Each has been criticized as too regressive and as too progressive. Proposals have been made to replace each major type of tax with another type of tax.

History

Federal Tax Receipts as a Percentage of GDP

U.S. federal government tax receipts as a percentage of GDP from 1945 to 2015

(note that 2010 to 2015 data are estimated)

Is it any wonder that Congress can't keep track of their spending? If you had an income stream like they have to handle, you'd feel the way they do like you couldn't ever spend it all.

So how do we handle all this money? Maybe one

alternative could be Direct Democracy.

Now let's take a look at Direct Democracy: (Excerpted from Wikipedia)

History:

The earliest known direct democracy is said to be the Athenian democracy in the 5th century BC, although it may be argued that it was not a liberal democracy because women, foreigners and slaves were excluded from it. The main bodies in the Athenian democracy were the assembly, composed by male citizens, the boule, composed by 500 citizens chosen annually by lot, and the law courts composed by a massive number of juries chosen by lot, with no judges. Out of the male population of 30,000, several thousand citizens were politically active every year and many of them quite regularly for years on end. The Athenian democracy was not only *direct* in the sense decisions were made by the assembled people, but also in the sense that the people through the assembly, boule and law courts controlled the entire political process and a large proportion of citizens were involved constantly in the public business. Modern democracies do not use institutions that resemble the Athenian system of rule. (note: We might want to relook at the way they did their democratic business back it's possible we could something from the inventers of democracy.)

Also relevant is the history of Roman republic beginning circa 449 BC. The ancient Roman Republic's "citizen lawmaking" – citizen formulation and passage of law, as well as citizen veto of legislature-made law – began about 449 BC and lasted the approximately 400 years to the death of Julius Caesar in 44 BC. Many historians mark the end of the Republic on the passage of a law named the Lex Titia, 27 November 43 BC.

Modern-era citizen lawmaking began in the towns of Switzerland in the 13th century. In 1847, the Swiss added the "statute referendum" to their national constitution. They soon discovered that merely having the power to veto Parliament's laws was not enough. In 1891, they added the "constitutional amendment initiative". The Swiss political battles since 1891 have given the world a valuable experience base with the national-level constitutional amendment initiative (Kobach, 1993). In the past 120 years, more than 240 initiatives have been put to referendum. The populace has been conservative, approving only about 10% of these initiatives; in addition, they have often opted for a version of the initiative rewritten by government. Another example is the United States, where, despite being a federal republic where no direct democracy exists at the federal level, almost half the states (and many localities) provide for citizen-sponsored ballot initiatives (also called "ballot measures" or "ballot questions") and the vast majority of the states have either initiatives and/or referendums.

A new technological communications called e-democracy often referred to as *electronic direct democracy*. More concisely, the concept of open source governance applies principles of the free software movement to the governance of people, allowing the entire populace to participate in government directly, as much or as little as they please. This development strains the traditional concept of democracy, because it does not necessarily give equal representation to each person. Some implementations may even be considered democratically-inspired meritocracies, where contributors to the code of laws are given preference based on their ranking by other contributors.

Direct Democracy Trilemma

Democratic theorists have identified a trilemma due to the presence of three desirable characteristics of an ideal system of direct democracy, which are challenging to deliver all at once. These three characteristics are *participation* - widespread participation in the decision making process by the people effected; *deliberation* - a rational discussion where all major points of view are weighted according to evidence; and *equality* - all members of the population on whose behalf decisions are taken have an equal chance of having their views taken into account. Empirical evidence from dozens of studies suggests deliberation leads to better decision making. However, the more participants there are the more time and money is needed to set up good quality discussions with clear neutrally presented briefings. Also it is hard for each individual to contribute substantially to the discussion when large numbers are involved. For the system to respect the principle of political equality, either *everyone* needs to be involved or there needs to be a representative random sample of people chosen to take part in the discussion. In the definition used by scholars such as James Fiskin, deliberative democracy is a form of direct democracy which satisfies the requirement for deliberation and equality but does not make provision to involve everyone who wants to be included in the discussion. Participatory democracy, by Fiskin's definition, allows inclusive participation and deliberation, but at a cost of sacrificing equality - because widespread participation is allowed there will rarely be sufficient resources to compensate people who give up their time to take part in the deliberation, and so the participants tend to be those with a strong interest in the issue to be decided, and therefore will often not be representative of the overall population. Fiskin instead argues that random sampling should be used to select a small but still representative number of people from the general public.

Fiskin concedes it is possible to imagine a system that transcends the trilemma, but it would require very radical reforms if such a system is to be integrated into mainstream politics. To an extent the Occupy movement has attempted to create a system that satisfies all three desirable requirements at once, but at a cost of the resulting system being widely criticized for being slow and unwieldy. [1]

Examples:

Ancient Athens

Athenian democracy developed in the Greek city-state, comprising the central city-state of Athens and the surrounding territory of Attica, around 500 BC. Athens was one of the very first known democracies. Other Greek cities set up democracies, and even though most followed an Athenian model, none were as powerful, stable, or as well-documented as that of Athens. In that direct democracy the people did not elect representatives to vote on their behalf but vote on legislation and executive bills in their own right. Participation was by no means open, but the in-group of participants was constituted with no reference to economic class and they participated on a big scale. The public opinion of voters was remarkably influenced by the political satire performed by the comic poets at the theaters

Solon (594 BC), Cleistenes (508/7 BC), and Ephialtes (462 BC) all contributed to the development of Athenian democracy. Historians differ on which of them was responsible for which institution, and which of them most represented a truly democratic movement. It is most usual to date Athenian democracy from Cleisthenes, since

Solon's constitution fell and was replaced by the tyranny of Peistratus, whereas Ephialtes revised Cleisthenes' constitution relatively peacefully. Hipparcus, the brother of the tyrant Hippias, was killed by Harmodius and Aristogeiton, who were subsequently honored by the Athenians for their alleged restoration of Athenian freedom.

The greatest and longest lasting democratic leader was Pericles;; after his death, Athenian democracy was twice briefly interrupted by oligarchic revolution towards the end of the Peloponnesian War. It was modified somewhat after it was restored under Eucleides; the most detailed accounts are of this fourth-century modification rather than the Periclean system. It was suppressed by the Macedonians in 322 BC. The Athenian institutions were later revived, but the extent to which they were a real democracy is debatable.

Switzerland

In Switzerland, single majorities are sufficient at the town, city, and canton (county)level, but at the national level, double majorities are required on constitutional matters. The intent of the double majorities is simply to ensure any citizen-made law's legitimacy (Kobach, 1993).

Double majorities are, first, the approval by a majority of those voting, and, second, a majority of cantons in which a majority of those voting approve the ballot measure. A citizen-proposed law (i.e. initiative) cannot be passed in Switzerland at the national level if a majority of the people approve but a majority of the cantons disapprove (Kobach, 1993). For referendums or propositions in general terms (like the principle of a general revision of the Constitution), the majority of those voting is enough (Swiss constitution, 2005).

In 1890, when the provisions for Swiss national citizen lawmaking were being debated by civil society and government, the Swiss adopted the idea of double majorities from the United States Congress, in which House votes were to represent the people and Senate votes were to represent the states (Kobach, 1993). According to its supporters, this "legitimacy-rich" approach to national citizen lawmaking has been very successful. Kobach claims that Switzerland has had tandem successes both socially and economically which are matched by only a few other nations. Kobach states at the end of his book, "Too often, observers deem Switzerland an oddity among political systems. It is more appropriate to regard it as a pioneer." Finally, the Swiss political system, including its direct democratic devices in a multi-level governance context, becomes increasingly interesting for scholars of European Union integration (see Trechsel, 2005)

United States

Direct democracy was very much opposed by the framers of the United States Constitution and some signatories of the Declaration of Independence. They saw a danger in majorities forcing their will on minorities. As a result, they advocated a representative democracy[1] in the form of a constitutional republic over a direct democracy. For example, James Madison, in Federalist No. 10 advocates a constitutional republic over direct democracy precisely to protect the individual from the will of the majority. He says, "A pure democracy can admit no cure for the mischiefs of faction. A common passion or interest will be felt by a majority, and there is nothing to check the inducements to sacrifice the weaker party. Hence it is, that democracies have ever been found incompatible with personal security or the rights of property; and have, in general, been as short in their lives as they have been violent in their deaths. "John Witherspoon, one of the signers of the Declaration of Independence, said "Pure democracy cannot subsist long nor be carried far into the departments of state – it is very subject to caprice and the madness of popular rage." Alexander Hamilton said, "That a pure democracy if it were practicable would be the most perfect government. Experience has proved that no position is more false than this. The ancient democracies in which the people themselves deliberated never possessed one good feature of government. Their very character was tyranny; their figure, deformity."

Despite the framers' intentions in the beginning of the republic, ballot measures and their corresponding referendums have been widely used at the state and sub-state level. There is much state and federal case law, from the early 1900s to the 1990s, that protects the people's right to each of these direct democracy governance components (Magleby, 1984, and Zimmerman, 1999). The first United States Supreme Court ruling in favor of the citizen lawmaking was in *Pacific States Telephone and Telegraph Company v. Oregon*, 223 U.S. 118 in 1912 (Zimmerman, December 1999). President Theodore Roosevelt, in his "Charter of Democracy" speech to the 1912 Ohio constitutional convention, stated "I believe in the Initiative and Referendum, which should be used not to destroy representative government, but to correct it whenever it becomes misrepresentative."

In various states, referendums through which the people rule include:[1]

- *Referrals* by the legislature to the people of "proposed constitutional amendments" (constitutionally used in 49 states, excepting only Delaware – Initiative & Referendum Institute, 2004).
- *Referrals* by the legislature to the people of "proposed statute laws" (constitutionally used in all 50 states – Initiative & Referendum Institute, 2004).
- *Constitutional amendment initiative* is the most powerful citizen-initiated, direct democracy governance component.[1] It is a constitutionally-defined petition process of "proposed constitutional law", which, if successful, results in its provisions being written directly into the state's constitution. Since constitutional law cannot be altered by state legislatures, this direct democracy component gives the people an automatic superiority and sovereignty, over representative government (Magelby, 1984). It is utilized at the state level in eighteen states: Arizona, Arkansas, California, Colorado, Florida, Illinois, Massachusetts, Michigan, Mississippi, Missouri, Montana, Nebraska, Nevada, North Dakota, Ohio, Oklahoma, Oregon and South Dakota (Cronin, 1989). Among the eighteen states, there are three main types of the constitutional amendment initiative, with different degrees of involvement of the state legislature distinguishing between the types (Zimmerman, December 1999).
- *Statute law initiative* is a constitutionally-defined, citizen-initiated, petition process of "proposed statute law", which, if successful, results in law being written directly into the state's statutes. The statute initiative is used at the state level in twenty-one states: Alaska, Arizona, Arkansas, California, Colorado, Idaho, Maine, Massachusetts, Michigan, Missouri, Montana,

Nebraska, Nevada, North Dakota, Ohio, Oklahoma, Oregon, South Dakota, Utah, Washington and Wyoming (Cronin, 1989). Note that, in Utah, there is no constitutional provision for citizen lawmaking. All of Utah's I&R law is in the state statutes (Zimmerman, December 1999). In most states, there is no special protection for citizen-made statutes; the legislature can begin to amend them immediately.

- *Statute law referendum* is a constitutionally-defined, citizen-initiated, petition process of the "proposed veto of all or part of a legislature-made law", which, if successful, repeals the standing law. It is used at the state level in twenty-four states: Alaska, Arizona, Arkansas, California, Colorado, Idaho, Kentucky, Maine, Maryland, Massachusetts, Michigan, Missouri, Montana, Nebraska, Nevada, New Mexico, North Dakota, Ohio, Oklahoma, Oregon, South Dakota, Utah, Washington and Wyoming (Cronin, 1989).

- The *recall* is a constitutionally-defined, citizen-initiated, petition process, which, if successful, removes an elected official from office by "recalling" the official's election. In most state and sub-state jurisdictions having this governance component, voting for the ballot that determines the recall includes voting for one of a slate of candidates to be the next office holder, if the recall is successful. It is utilized at the state level in nineteen states: Alaska, Arizona, California, Colorado, Georgia, Idaho, Illinois, Kansas, Louisiana, Michigan, Minnesota, Montana, Nevada, New Jersey, North Dakota, Oregon, Rhode Island, Washington and Wisconsin (National Conference of State Legislatures, 2011, Recall of State Officials).

There are now a total of 24 U.S. states with constitutionally-defined, citizen-initiated, direct democracy governance components (Zimmerman, December 1999). In the United States, for the most part only one-time majorities are required (simple majority of those voting) to approve any of these components.[1]

In addition, many localities around the U.S. also provide for some or all of these direct democracy governance components, and in specific classes of initiatives (like those for raising taxes), there is a super majority voting threshold requirement. Even in states where direct democracy components are scant or nonexistent at the state level, there often exists local options for deciding specific issues, such as whether a county should be "wet" or "dry" in terms of whether alcohol sales are allowed.

In the U.S. region of New England, many municipalities practice a very limited form of home rule, and decide local affairs through the direct democratic process of the town meeting

Electronic Direct Democracy

Electronic direct democracy (EDD), also known as Direct Digital Democracy (DDD) or E-democracy, is a form of direct democracy which utilizes telecommunications to facilitate public participation. Electronic direct democracy is sometimes referred to by other names, such as open source governance and collaborative governance.

EDD requires electronic voting or some way to register votes on issues electronically. As in any direct democracy, in an EDD, citizens would have the right to vote on legislation, author new legislation, and recall representatives (if any representatives are preserved).

Technology for supporting EDD has been researched and developed at the Florida Institute of Technology where the technology is used with student organizations. Numerous other software development projects are underway, along with many supporting and related projects. Several of these projects are now collaborating on a cross-platform architecture, under the umbrella of the Meta-government project.

EDD as a system is not fully implemented in a political government anywhere in the world, although several initiatives are currently forming. Ross Perot was a prominent advocate of EDD when he advocated "electronic town halls" during his 1992 and 1996 Presidential campaigns in the United States. Switzerland, already partially governed by direct democracy, is making progress towards such a system. Senate Online, an Australian political party running for the Senate in the 2007 federal elections, proposed to institute an EDD system so that Australians can decide which way the senators vote on each and every bill. A similar initiative was formed 2002 in Sweden where the party Aktivdemokrati, running for the Swedish parliament, offers its members the power to decide the actions of the party over all or some areas of decision, or alternatively to use a proxy with immediate recall for one or several areas. Since early 2011 EDD parties are working together on the Participedia wiki E2D

The first mainstream direct democracy party to be registered with any country's electoral commission (checked against each country's register) is the UK's People's Administration Direct Democracy party. The People's Administration have developed and published the complete architecture for a legitimate reform to EDD (including the required Parliamentary reform process). Established by musicians ([including Alex Romane) and

168

political activists, the People's Administration advocates using the web and telephone to enable the majority electorate to create, propose and vote upon all policy implementation. The People's Administration's blueprint has been published in various forms since 1998 and the People's Administration is the first direct democracy party registered in a vote-able format anywhere in the world - making transition possible through evolution via election with legitimate majority support, instead of potentially through revolution via violence. This is along the lines or which we are moving with this books suggestions. However, the completed idea is waiting to be developed by the National Committee for the resurrection of our republic.

So would an Electronic form of Direct Democracy be an alternative management tool for today? I say we take a close look at the potential. Yes, there are people who think it's too risky to try, but I say with the Internet being much more sophisticated and secure than in the past it might be time to develop a system that could work to our advantage. This would give the ordinary citizen much more input into the way the government does things. As stated in the article, many states in the US are already testing these theories and they seem to be working well. Why not implement the system on a Federal level and have more direct effect on the running of our government.

Chapter 8 – The Plan

So now we have a theory for redesigning our form of Government. Why do we need to worry about this in the first place? Let me count the ways.

The first situation we need to be cognizant of is what is government's job? We can all agree that according to Aristotle the best form of government (Republic) should have as its goal governing the people in such a way as to provide the majority of the populous with as much happiness as possible.

Cicero of Rome stated:
The role of the statesman (*rector rei publicae*) is to aim at the happiness of the citizens, defined in a laxer way than most Greek philosophers would allow, as wealth, glory, and virtue all combined.

That's not being accomplished by our present Federal Government. By direction through our own Constitution that states:

*We hold these truths to be self-evident, that all men are created equal, that they are endowed by their Creator with certain unalienable Rights, that among these are Life, Liberty and the pursuit of Happiness. That to secure these rights, Governments are instituted among Men, deriving their just powers from the consent of the governed, **That whenever any Form of Government becomes destructive of these ends, it is the Right of the People to alter or to abolish it, and to institute new Government, laying its foundation on such principles and organizing its powers*** *in such form, as to them shall seem most likely to affect their Safety and Happiness*.(This is the part that needs redressing today) *Prudence, indeed, will dictate that Governments long established should not be changed for light and transient causes; and accordingly all experience hath shewn, that mankind are more disposed to suffer, while evils are sufferable, than to right themselves by abolishing the forms to which they are accustomed. But when a long train of abuses and usurpations, pursuing invariably the same Object evinces a design to reduce them under absolute Despotism, it is their right, it is their duty, to throw off such Government, and to provide new Guards for their future security.* (This excerpt being taken word for word, from the Declaration of Independence, Chapter 2) Which tells us that if the government we have is not performing its duties as a representation of the majority of the peoples than we as the population of the United States have the Right to alter or abolish the present government and implement a new system that more rightly conforms to the needs of the majority of the people. However, we were warned that this power should not be taken frivolously but with great care, but if needed our forefathers built into the Constitution a lawful way to go about completing this requirement.

This treatise lays out the precise steps that need to be legally performed to accomplish our requirements. In this chapter we will cover the steps required in a logical manner in order that we can achieve our goals with a minimum amount of grief and as calmly as is possible. It's known, however, there will be some pain associated with the inevitable changes which will take place. The key is to make the transition as painlessly as possible. People will be hurt, many will lose their job, some will lose their career, but if the moves are made judiciously, keeping in mind that people are impacted by the changes made, then we can institute these changes in a manner so as to minimize the psychological and physical stress on the majority of affected workers.

What we will need to always keep in mind are the needs of the affected people. We need to keep in mind that the Government didn't get in this condition overnight nor do we have to make these changes over night. We can plan our implementation over time so as to give those effected sufficient time to make plans for their transition. A good example of people who are trapped by Government Laws and systems is our Senior population. These unsuspecting people have paid into a system (Social Security)which was doomed to fail. Why? Because these Politicians abused the money that was given to them for the express reason of providing for these folk's retirement. Well the unscrupulous usurpers spent the money given to them, money that was contributed for a specific reason and the politicians used that money for any number of reasons having nothing to do with the retirement years for those people.

These politicians used the money in their Pork Barrel projects for the express reason of fattening their own pockets. Now…when our seniors need this money they willingly contributed, these same Congressmen and women claim the money isn't there, they claim the program wasn't properly funded.

172

I say we need to respect the rights of these seniors and continue to pay them what they have earned until the last participants have died then close the system. Yes it will cost some money and pain but they made a deal with the Regime who promised them a secure retirement but then duped these seniors into giving up their hard earned money (basically an extra tax) so the Government could use this contributed money for their nefarious dealings. They trusted their Government to guard their money and have it ready to distribute to them when they needed it. Well we need to honor that commitment.

So I say let's keep the contracts with people who stand to lose their livelihoods through the shady dealings of these past Governments and make our changes going forward. It will be harder and take a lot more time but if this were being done for a family household, we would have to meet our present obligations and try to implement our reorganization plan within the current conditions. That is the way I would approach this situation as well.

This is the attitude we need to take when dealing with all programs currently in place with the present Government. Our people have grown used to the crooked night time closed door dealings that is currently being done in our Government today and this "Modus Operandi" is explained to us as "The way to get things done in these days and times." I say that's just so much bunk. The current group of Senators and Representatives are just trying to feed the American people a bunch of propaganda the same way other Regimes of the past tried to sell this same story to their people. Eventually the people of the past didn't take their crap either and we should not believe what our government people say now.

We need to start immediately to effect change within the government by using the tools we have been given to voice our opinion as to how our system should work, and use those tools to make the changes needed to bring about the necessary modifications we see as required to bring our government system back to one that's attuned to the needs of the majority of the people, not to the thieves and connivers of the current form of government.

Remember these words: ***That whenever any Form of Government becomes destructive of these ends, it is the Right of the People to alter or to abolish it, and to institute new Government, laying its foundation on such principles and organizing its powers in such form, as to them shall seem most likely to affect their Safety and Happiness***. This is directly from the Declaration of Independence and it speaks directly to what is currently going on today. Read carefully what it's telling us to do.

This is <u>exactly</u> what they are telling us to do: *Prudence, indeed, will dictate that Governments long established should not be changed for light and transient causes; and accordingly all experience hath shown, that mankind are more disposed to suffer, while evils are sufferable, than to right themselves by abolishing the forms to which they are accustomed. But when a long train of abuses and usurpations, pursuing invariably the same Object evinces a design to reduce them under absolute Despotism, it is their right, it is their duty, to throw off such Government, and to provide new Guards for their future security.*

So, there you have it…it couldn't be any plainer than that. We need to take charge of our own destiny and make the changes we see as necessary…now!

How do we make those changes? We don't want to cause insurrection and strife, that's not necessary. We have other means at our disposal. Through the democratic process we can make the changes we need to make legally and peacefully.

One of the first cautions I would offer is to stay away from the current Political machines. They are corrupt and ensconced in the "way things have always been done here" mindset. We don't need their opinion or direction. Being part of the problem allowing them to input any opinion will only corrupt our efforts and slow the process. The political system we have now should be, in my opinion, completely dismantled and rebuilt by fresh thinkers, people who are thinking about how people want the new system to operate not perpetuate more of the same.

Next we should install the system we discussed earlier in this book.

We will need to organize a 2nd Constitutional Convention Commission that will oversee the reorganization of the Federal Government. Reorganized in this manner:

This Commission will use our new theories from running a profitable business, there is an axiom in business that states, "All business has a useful life which emulates human life". There is a birth, a period of growth, a maturing process, followed by old age (infirmity) and finally death.   The term used by most business theorists is Organizational Life. So right now you are probably thinking…so what that's nothing new. If we were only talking about human life you would be exactly right, however, in the case of organizational life is not precisely the same. The way organizational life developed was a bit unique from physical life. We use the same life development cycles, but we have the ability to prolong life indefinitely.

(Reprinted from Chapter 5)
Here's how it works. Let's say we decide to go into a business, just for sake of explanation we will call it a widget business. Widgets are a good example as they don't exist and we don't have to have people telling us that we are operating our business improperly. After all, this is only an example to be used for clarification.

We get together a nucleus of people, and in the beginning we recruit several experts in the manufacturing and operation of widgets. We are determined to put together the finest widget research that money can produce. We have researched other widget manufacturers and are satisfied that our product is the best on the market today. So with much excitement we begin.

Our first steps will be tenuous at best. In this start-up phase, we begin our process, but there are a million questions…are we adequately financed? Are our processes correct? Can we find enough customers to make us successful? And so on. So after we suffer through this tenuous time we emerge successful we have weathered the onslaught from the competition and we are ensconced in the business of building great widgets and have become a factor in the Widget industry.

Now, the next and most exciting stage…Exponential growth. If we survive the start-up stage and with our acceptance into the industry, gain a place to sell our product, we will enter into the stage called momentum. We attain our deserved reputation of quality and innovative approach of the widgets produced by our company and we are dominating the industry. Now we grow in leaps and bounds. We are enjoying huge amounts of profit and market growth. With our new found profitability we engage in a period of expansion. We build new plants and distribution centers all over the world. We are at the top of our game. So we are enjoying our success. We may even increase the salaries and benefits of the principals within the company. We may even over hire a few relatives to "take care" of our families. Of course they deserve their rewards; they stuck with us in the lean times.

We have become inarguably the top of our industry. The unchallenged behemoth of all widget companies in the world at this time. So we settle in and prepare to enjoy our well-deserved rewards for all our hard work, sweat and tears. This will continue for a period of time, a time where we will live on our laurels, so to speak. During this time we will continue to produce an acceptable amount of widgets and the quality will remain the same or, because of an influx of less than interested new company employees who may only be in the company to garner a great paycheck and may not be as interested in the quality of the product as we once were, the quality may have deteriorated slightly, but we are still doing ok. Profitability is there and we still have the majority of our loyal customer base, but for some reason we haven't been growing as fast lately. What's happened is the original crew, at least most of them, have moved on in one way or another and the replacements are not what you would call overly excited about producing great widgets they're more interested in the getting the great money and benefits they are getting by having their position in the company. (This is called the "Maturity" stage).

Then, out of the blue, appears a new bunch of young guns (A lot like we were years ago). A new group of engineers who have come together and developed a new digitized widget, this product is not only better, faster and smaller than our conventional widget, but it's cheaper to make and it lasts longer. We are devastated. In a matter of weeks or maybe months we have lost our customer base, and our widget has gone the way of the buggy whip. We don't have anyone in the company who knows anything about digital processes and can't seem to find anyone who is willing to work with us until we can get up to speed. We finally realize that if we don't get up to speed on technology we will be forced to file for bankruptcy. So we see the demise of our illustrious widget company.

That is, as I'm sure you realized, the life cycle of a business (at least an example of one). The same life cycle happens

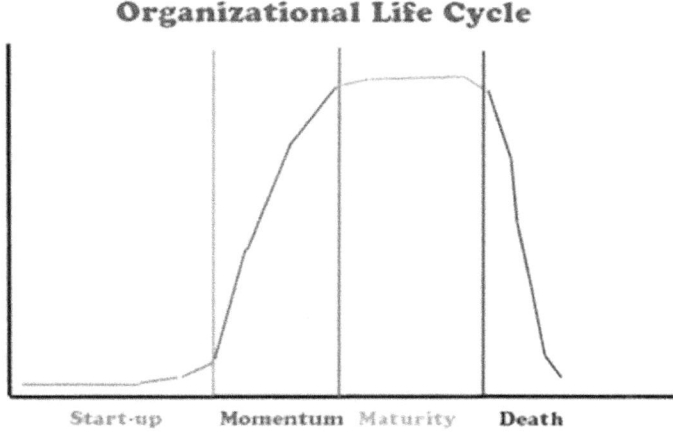

Organizational Life Cycle

Start-up   Momentum   Maturity   Death

to all entities, human, biological, business, and government. For the last two, however, it doesn't need to be that way. There are methodologies available that if used expeditiously can breathe new life into the business or government entity and that entity is able to extend its life indefinitely. Next we will take a look at how we can accomplish that phenomenon.

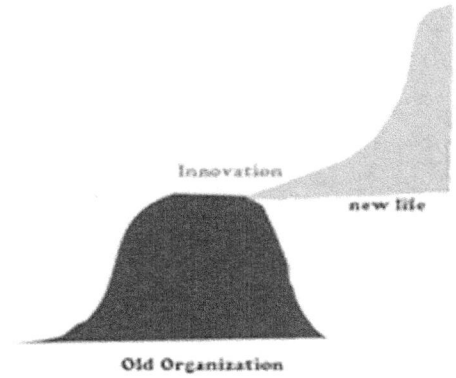

Innovation

new life

Old Organization

What we are looking to do for the reorganization of the government is to enter into the Organizational Life Cycle at the late Maturity Stage and add onto the Organizational Life Cycle another "Start Up Cycle" to enable the Life Cycle to begin again. By doing this additional step we effectively restart the Life Cycle to extend the life of the entity (here being the Federal Government) indefinitely. This is done by monitoring the Organizational Life Cycle and when it's determined to again be entering the Death Cycle we simply reconvene a Committee and reassess the process and make updates to the system.

The process is simple enough, but the present government employees won't be too cooperative with this process because it may mean the loss of their job. Keep in mind that each and every time this process is used it may cause some changes in the way the government operates, meaning that someone may be hurt each and every time this process is used to refine the government. Keep in mind though, if we want an efficient and well working government that is keeping up with the needs of the people than this is the best process to use.

Keep in mind we will have to finance this effort through contributions from people who are dedicated to seeing this program develop a new more efficient system of governance. To facilitate this process I'm setting up a website that will be accepting donations expressly to finance day to day operations. HTTP://resurrecting therepublic.org

So now we know the answer as to how to keep our government up to our standards of efficiency and economics, but how do we pull it off without violence and pain?

One State at a time…well, not literally, but organizing State level organizations can start posturing much like the Tea Party did to reorganize the State Legislature and begin working on the planned restructuring that will be necessary to cause the needed changes to the Federal Governmental System.

According to Aristotle, the government should be the "body and soul" of the people. Through critical thought I would understand that to mean the government would be aware of our wants and needs and react to those needs in a comprehensive way so as to meet the needs of the majority of the citizens while being attuned to the freedoms of all and negotiating the best possible situation in which the populous can function. The only way to create this "body and soul" form of government is to organize it in such a way so as to respond quickly to the needs of the local population. A local government who can listen to and react to the changing needs of its local populous.

The next situation which needs attention within the Aristotle definition is the fact the government is not being run efficiently or effectively by "craftsmen" and it's not, in any way, fulfilling the people's final desire's or needs. In fact, it appears, by all intents and purposes, to be the antithesis of fulfilling any of the people's needs or wants, the government now seems to be passing legislation to satisfy their personal agendas.

So the idea that politicians should be craftsmen is not applicable to our Congressmen. They are instead, as least it seems to me, professional thieves. They go to College for the express purpose of becoming professional politicians. Why would a person go to school to study Politics except to become a Congressman or governmental manager? Craftsmen are not "Professionals" they are highly trained artisans, people who intern for years to become adept at their craft and their craft does not have to necessarily be politics. One of the major imperfections in our Congress is we do, in fact, have too many professional politicians, these politicians have no experience in any other subjects in which people may have needs. They are passing laws on transportation, medicine, public safety, education, etc. All these congressional professionals of today know is how to draft a bill. They are, nearly to a man, all Lawyers. I ask you how does a Lawyer know how to respond to the needs of a Plumber or Mechanic?

So how I feel is that we need to design a Federal Government that is aware of our local needs and can respond quickly to what the present situation is. That needs to be done at the lowest level.

What we will use as our tool for reformation is:

Amendment 10 - Powers of the States and People. Ratified 12/15/1791.

"The powers not delegated to the United States by the Constitution, nor prohibited by it to the States, are reserved to the States respectively, or to the people."

Note this well. Anything not expressly granted to the Federal government is reserved for the States or the People. Although this amendment is very liberally interpreted, it is one of the tenets of the Constitution. This amendment is also known as the States' Rights Amendment.

Keeping in mind the "Organizational Life Cycle" theory, we should realize the present governmental process is in its final stage of this process and demands reassessment. With this in mind, the several states that will form the Coalition will have to act to curtail the powers of the federal government. Here's the suggested plan:

After the organizing of the Coalition, a series of committees would be formed to assess the functionality of each department, division, agency or office within, controlled by or any part of the federal government, in other words every entity of the federal government. Everything they have anything to do with needs to be examined and after being scrutinized by a group or several groups, it must be determined through the criteria developed by the Coalition, if the entity is viable or not. Does it function efficiently? Is it accomplishing a useful purpose? Is it redundant? Is it viable and timely? Does it need updating? Can it be replaced with a system that is more effective and easier to implement?

I'm sure there are many more questions to ask, but they will be up to the Second Federal Constitutional Convention Commission to determine. The most important aspect of this treatise is to critically look at the machinations of the Federal Government and determine as to its viability. Is the current system current and functioning efficiently and effectively without redundancy. Is the system needed in the federal scheme of things or could the service be better managed by the states.

The Plan

The first requirement will be to organize a Second Federal Constitutional Convention Commission. This can be done in several ways. My suggestion is to organize on the Internet (**http://www.resurrectingtherepublic.org**). I will develop a website that will service our needs temporarily. One of the artisans I will be looking for will be a Webmaster to manage the site.

Once we get an organized Second Federal Constitutional Convention then this Committee can determine how they wish to proceed from there. Initially I don't think brick and mortar is needed, but we will need funding, a Marketing specialist and a Web Master. The funding goes without saying, without the money all the theory in the world will never happen. One thing we must insist upon is that the money is given with the understanding that it is given without reservation and with the understanding there will be no special consideration on anything we do. This will not become another PAC that exists on donations that have strings attached. The only reason to give to our cause will be the giver wants to see the United States become what it once was... the greatest power in the world, a nation that will be a shining example for the rest of the world to emulate. Next we need to find a Marketing Specialist who will give their time to get this program off and running. Someone who will develop a marketing campaign that will generate interest in the cause and help generate people and money to bring our plan to fruition and finally a good Web

Master who can design and maintain the website we will need to get our story out to the public. Finally all resources will remain totally transparent. This is going to be an above-board effort that will remain reviewable on a continuing basis.

With proper management we can get things organized through digital media. Of course care must be taken to safe guard our site from whatever attacks spring up, but it is the same with any endeavor placed on public media and it may have the further benefit of having a good way to keep us in contact with the public. The site should be open and totally accessible to all. The public should have access to view all information and be invited to leave suggestions and feedback.

The next step will be to start organizing individual state committees keeping in mind that we will need to have state committees for each state. The Second Federal Constitutional Convention can design the requirements for a state committee complying with Constitutional law to be able to get started with its primary function, which will be to start investigating all the Departments, Agencies and Offices of the Federal Government and developing their reports on their findings and recommendations for changing the system.

Organizing and maintaining these organizations will be the most difficult challenge in this entire plan. I will start by organizing and designing a website dedicated to this plan. It will serve as a clearing house for all countrywide information that will be necessary to keep things running smoothly.

You may feel that the hardest part of this plan will be the opposition we will get from the current system, I don't think so. My feeling is that our biggest challenge will come from our own ranks. Keeping everyone motivated and focused on the mission will be by far the most difficult task. In the beginning people get enthused and excited about a new idea and will do the tasks with gusto and zeal, however, as the process moves along and the tasks become more difficult or some amount of patience is required, some of us will lose interest. The committed ones will remain focused on the goal and will move the process along and ensure that the process is brought to fruition. This will be accomplished by setting up an initial set of goals and manage our work by developing a plan to meet those goals.

What we need to accomplish has never been done before. We will be calling for a Constitutional Convention. There is no provision for the holding of referendums at the federal level in the United States; indeed, there is no national electorate of any kind. The United States Constitution does not provide for referendums at the federal level. A Constitutional Amendment would be required to allow it. However, the Constitutions of 24 states (principally in the West) and many local and city governments provide for referendums and citizen's initiatives.

A Constitutional Convention can be called by two-thirds of the legislatures of the States, and that Convention to propose one or more amendments to the Constitution. These amendments are then sent to the states to be approved by three-fourths of the legislatures or conventions. This route has never been taken, and there is discussion in political science circles about just how such a convention would be convened, and what kind of changes it would bring about.

So it begins here and now. With this small book, it isn't very long, but it says so much. Will it be easy? Probably not, is it needed…I think so that's why I'm writing this now. So let's get this thing started so we can reap some of the rewards. Let's make this country into what it once was or maybe even better.

It goes without saying that we will need funding and any volunteers who feel as strongly as I do about this imperative. So if fall into any category that you think I would be interested in you or your views All you need to do is contact me at: chuck@resurrectingtherepublic.org, http:/www.resurrectingthe republic.org or http://resurrectingtherepublic.com